Praise for *A Garden of Black Joy*

"*A Garden of Black Joy*, more than any collection I've read, made me understand and remix Margaret Walker's insistent plea that we write to and for our people. This work is liberation, not just liberatory, which means it dutifully holds our brokenness, our longing, and our sensual satisfaction like a secret. Then it tells. And we listen because these Black poets chose us

lese Laymon, author of
Heavy: An American Memoir

D1564110

"These poems articulate the banal, the ..... .ul, the fantastic, and the everyday joy in the lives of black people around the world. In doing so, they evince a compelling vision of possibilities otherwise."

—Shannon Gibney,
author of *Dream Country*

"The task that has confronted and at times confounded black folks since we were called 'black' is to envision and enact a world beyond perception, a transcendent world that defies the humanity we were created outside of. The work of the scholar/poet is to lead us in this effort. I use the term scholar/poet because I am in search of the dialectical space that Keno Evol inhabits. For those of us who have had the fortune to know Keno, *A Garden of Black Joy* is of no surprise because he has been conjuring worlds for and with us in the fiercest way possible—with joy and love. Keno has managed to make joy a world, which he calls us to enter, to perhaps make a joyful noise. In this world he uncovers the hideous and deconstructs the grotesque, rendering them as mere distractions in the pursuit of Black Joy. In this way, Evol stands in the tradition of Black Radical metaphysics, the domain of the maroon, who couldn't understand themselves as property, built another world, and sparked a fire for those who would pay attention to the smoke in the distance."

—Dr. Brian Lozenski, assistant professor
of urban and multicultural education,
Macalester College

"*A Garden of Black Joy*, curated by the unstoppable visionary Keno Evol, is exactly what this world needs now and into the future to keep bringing us back to the liberatory and fantastic visions of dystopia(s) and utopia(s). These have always been part of the radical Black prophetic tradition, as Evol so lovingly traces in his brilliant and moving introduction, a work of art in and of itself. The works in this anthology testify to the conditions of Black life, which, as articulated by Black writers such as Audre Lorde and Toni Morrison and so many more, have always demanded the poetics of citizenship of another world within, without, sideways, backwards, and forward from the ongoing (neo)colonial world of racial capitalism and other violences against Black bodies, spirits, and imaginations. This underground must simultaneously be lived within the individual, in the present, and intergenerationally, as a form of fugitivity, as contemporary poets such as Chaun Webster and Fred Moten and many more have mapped. This living treasure, this changeling speculative work, *A Garden of Black Joy*, is manifestation of poetry as a deep ethics, a commitment to decolonialism (often beginning and ending with the body), and the infinitely sacred beauty of Black life on its own terms. Add this to the canon of the cosmos. It must be read, shared, taught, and lived by all of us who care about enacting a true moral commons. Those of us who are not Black, who benefit from the spoils of regimes of anti-Blackness, should find it our duty and our pleasure to encounter this powerful politics of beauty. Furious flowers!"

—신 선 영 辛善英 **Sun Yung Shin**,
award-winning author of *Unbearable Splendor*

"This collection is ancestoral and futuristic, and yet it gently ushers you into the present moment. It's serving all kinds of deliciousness. It's that before sunrise joy, that sing to the top of your lungs joy, that taking a deep breath joy, that fictive kinship joy, that #blackjoy."

—**Dr. Joi Lewis**, author of
Healing: The Act of Radical Self-Care

A GARDEN OF BLACK JOY

A GARDEN OF BLACK JOY

Global Poetry
from the Edges
of Liberation
and Living

Curated by Keno Evol

www.BlackTableArts.com

Minneapolis

ISBN 13: 978-1-63489-310-7
LCCN: 2019921081
Printed in the United States of America
First Printing: 2020

24 23 22 21 20   5 4 3 2 1

Cover illustration by Leslie Barlow
Cover and interior design by Patrick Maloney

Wise Ink Creative Publishing
807 Broadway St NE
Suite 46
Minneapolis, MN, 55413

To order, visit www.itascabooks.com or call 1-800-901-3480.
Reseller discounts available.

If you'd like to host an event for this collection,
email agardenofblackjoy@gmail.com

For my siblings.
To anyone black celebrating or hiding tucked
in a small place, sharing their joy.
For S'sense, a friend, mother, and poet,
who passed away too young—who would
describe what's gathered here as juicy.

Contents

If We Want Human Beings Alive in the Future, We Might Want to Listen to Poets

By Keno Evol

"This task that I am describing is not a task that even in principle could be performed within the existence of an individual."

—Roberto Unger, Harvard University School of Law

Welcome to *A Garden of Black Joy*. Thank you for picking up this book. It's a small project that I hope can be of use. There is a lot I would like to talk about in these first few pages, and because this is a book of poetry, it makes sense to begin at poetics. But I would also like to discuss more broadly the ways we engage community, art, love, liberation projects, the future, and the connections these might have to poetry.

Right now we have approximately eighty years until the twenty-second century, and it's not self-evident or obvious we'll get there as a species. I would like to see human beings alive in the future. For that, however, we need to make decisions collectively, and I believe poets can help.

Some of the thinkers I am going to be traveling with in this essay are poets, and some are not. Some are artists, and some are not. All of them position art as a resource that can be of use to those of us who are interested in the future.

I am a poet and educator doing organizing work in Minneapolis, Minnesota. I am the executive director of Black Table Arts, home to the Because Black Life Conference. Currently, most of my work involves political education and writing around ideas of the future and black utopias.

There are ways to think about the future just as there are ways to think about the idea of utopia, which I will go into later. For now, I will say that these concepts don't *really* exist. The idea of the future and the idea of utopia are only conceptual frameworks to think about the right here and right now. *How far do we have to go?* or *How much time do we have?*

1

The only way to think about the future is the only way to think about utopia: dialectically, putting two contrasting perspectives together. They do and they don't exist. We want to engage in this kind of thinking to answer the questions, *How are we living right now?* and *Who can we become in time?* What I am interested in thinking about with this collection are the connections between poetry, our relationship with land (particularly what we grow), and the future. Let's start with clear paths through this garden.

SMALL PATHWAYS THROUGH THE GARDEN— DIRECTIONS AND DEFINITIONS

What are poetics? Who is a poet? What exactly is poetry? How should we define a poem? Well, there are a few definitions that I love and use. My favorite definition of a poem comes from the *Oxford American Dictionary*: "a piece of writing that partakes in the nature of both speech and song."

Speech and song. I love this because it gets at an important ingredient in poetry: beauty. Beauty is a good ingredient toward possibility for any life form stuck in ruin. In this work I want to affirm black folks taking in beauty. For me, beauty in this respect does not necessarily mean *something pretty* but instead language that invokes vulnerability, which makes poems worth returning to.

Percy Shelley, the Romantic poet of the nineteenth century, wrote a ten-thousand-word essay described by educator and cultural critic Neil Postman as being "to intellectual life what the Declaration of Independence was to political life." The essay, titled "In the Defense of Poetry," defined poetry as the "expression of the imagination." I like this, and we will return to poetics and imagination later in the introduction.

When thinking about poetics, liberation work, and the future, it makes sense to begin at one of my favorite places, *the Fantastic*.

THE GARDEN & THE FANTASTIC

"The Fantastic" is a name given to a literary genre that presents to its readers or characters, usually through supernatural events, situations that make them hesitate and ask *Is this real?*—that duration of hesitation is called *the Fantastic.* What does this have to do with poetry? American literary critic Robert Scholes, describing the work of Bulgarian-French historian Tzvetan Todorov in the foreword to *The Fantastic: A Structural Approach to a Literary Genre*, says:

> Poetics is a liberating discipline, freeing us from the stifling norms of our own age and the past . . . that reduces texts to "classics" (squeezing the life out of them) and hinders our perception of the new unclassical or even anti-classical in literature.

> Poetics, we are told here, must serve to break down the barriers between the sacred . . . and the profane marketplace of popular culture. Poetics can help us see the literary quality in bumper stickers, or, conversely, the lack of literariness in the classics themselves. Poetics, truly understood, is a liberation from prejudice, an opening of the mind creating new opportunities for readers and writers.

Opening the mind and creating new opportunities. This largely speaks to what Black Table Arts is about, but we also want to take it further: we wish to provide, through art, new modes of gathering the public, particularly black folks living in Minnesota, to consider how we might live together inside and outside artistic spaces. We want to ask and then respond to the question, "What does the whole of this community look like?"

To once more highlight that first section, it says, "Poetics is a liberating discipline, freeing us from the stifling norms of our own age." Poetics as a way to say we don't have to live this way. When I think about *A Garden of Black Joy*, I am thinking about a collection of beautiful suggestions toward other possibilities. Or, in other words, providing our community chances to experience what we might call *the Black Fantastic.*

So in many ways, I think Scholes is correct. There are many places where the writers gathered here bring the Black Fantastic with them. In this anthology in particular, I am interested in the places where the poetic and the Black Fantastic meet. For example, when Ashley Davis, from Philadelphia, Pennsylvania, speaks about her grandmother in her poem "i learn time travel from Great Grandma Susie":

and SWOOSH! i watch my 95 year old Great Gramma turn 10
transport to her Gramma's living room with her baby sister
giggles tickling the flesh of their cheeks
sneaking sweets from somewhere

I love this, when grandmothers suddenly turn young at a moment's notice. These Black Fantastic moments where supernatural events and ordinary lives converge. These meetings of the Black Fantastic and the ordinary are where this anthology begins. A garden is where we can do these things. Or take another example, a poem by Olivia Dorsey Peacock from Dallas, Texas, "Beacon":

happiness was at the bottom
of an egg custard pie
where ferries sailed away

and to Beacon lights ice cream in hand
scuttling children leaping
thin brown bodies in thick coats on thick decks
to retreat to warm rooms

Here I want to push the fantastic further. I want to suggest that it isn't only a quality of hesitation to ask *Is this real?* or *Could this be real?* but also a quality of surprise. *I didn't know this could be possible*—and that is the essence of the Black Fantastic.

Surprise is where I want to connect the fantastic to joy. The moments of surprise in these poems are often also the moments where blackness meets joy. *and SWOOSH! i watch my 95 year old Great Gramma turn 10.*

This is another way of thinking about how to register the fantastic.

COMPLICATING JOY: JOY ISN'T ALWAYS JOYFUL

Though the fantastic, like joy, isn't always joyful. We hear this in a poem by Brittany Marshall from Baton Rouge, Louisiana, titled "they thought water and didn't think to think of us":

They didn't think our bodies would make it out/of the water/
because too much of anything can kill any   body except this/
                body/   filled/with so much surety/
the water begged for our forgiveness   and we don't mind
stepping out/   of ourselves/to conceive   of   ourselves/
we'll delight in the storm/and we'll rejoice in its carnage/because in
the morning/they'll wake up/with our scents/wafting from their
rubbish.

This is a completely different face of a joyful moment. Here we are
experiencing joy as a sort of bursting; an opening up. This joy is not
always joyful, but joy nonetheless. This idea of joy not always being
joyful has a kind of relationship to blackness. I would describe this as
a bursting under constraints. Experiences of rapture that can't be held
in or bounded. This anthology is interested in thinking about poetry
and poetics as a mode of literature pushing against and out from under
constraints to speak, write, and live out loud new possibilities toward the
future—again, the future being a conceptual container to think about
How are we living right now?

A POETIC VISION MAKES THE FUTURE DESIRABLE

What exactly is the future? How can we better understand it? Inside
Building a Bridge to the 18th Century, Neil Postman writes:

> The future is of course an illusion. Nothing has happened there yet . . . we may
> say of the future there is no *there* there . . . Imagined futures are always more
> about where we have been than where we are going . . . Kierkegaard is right
> in suggesting there is nothing to see in the future except something from the
> past, and he invites us to be quite careful about what part of the past we use in
> imagining the future.

What part of the past we use in imagining the future. This is import-
ant to sit with. When we consider this statement, what we are asking
ourselves is, *Are we learning from our history?* and *What goals do we want
for our future considering the history we come out of?* These questions are
often taken up in community spaces. One of these spaces that Black
Table Arts holds is the Because Black Life Conference, held annually at

different universities across the state of Minnesota. When I think about the work Because Black Life has been able to do as a gathering, I'm reminded of the poetry of Brittany Marshall, Olivia Dorsey Peacock, and Ashley Davis, whom I quoted above.

The Because Black Life Conference begins at the bottom of oceans, as Brittany Marshall tells us—as we know all too well from black historiographies, a location where there might be bodies. Bodies that were once living. Human beings. Our first time holding the Because Black Life Conference at the University of Minnesota in 2018, we got news that earlier in the day a community member had passed away. A community member who would have attended the conference. A friend to many who were in the room. A friend of mine, known to many as S'sence. A black woman. A mother. It was strange to be in two places at the same time. To figure out logistics and grief. Though in these moments, what you figure out is that you don't have to do it alone and you *can't* do it alone. We didn't. I didn't. Without it being scheduled or necessarily programed, we checked in on each other and made sure we were okay. This process is what we mean at Black Table Arts when we use the term *blackmosphere*.

In the book *The End of Night: Searching for Natural Darkness in an Age of Artificial Light*, Paul Bogard writes about Paris as the first city to pioneer this concept of a "light identity": "using light to create an atmosphere."

When we are thinking about *A Garden of Black Joy*, perhaps it is a place of blackmosphere. Where we find glowing, not only black identity, but a dark identity. Joachim Schlör describes, "This is the beauty of the night, a beauty 'rooted in atmosphere, that is not easily explained.'"

A blackmosphere where gardens grow. Not only as a space where art can be shared but as a space where, through political education, love, conviviality, and what we might call a *politics of regard*, we can decide the ethics under which we share. Some of these ethics lead to a "bursting" or an "opening up," some of which leads to what John Akomfrah describes within the careers of jazz artists as a "window of opportunity."

Both Black Table Arts and the Because Black Life Conference, along with what is gathered in this collection, are interested in various "windows of opportunity"—openings in spacetime where we have a chance to share and decide something. A chance to decide a direction for the future.

What does the future have to do with being a poet? Well, let's take a look at where these ideas of the future and poetry meet. On August 5, 2014, journalist Krista Tippett interviewed Harvard professor and philosopher Roberto Unger. She asks, "In the midst of all these lofty ideas, where does poetry come in?" He responds:

> It's vision. It's this ability that we have to look beyond this world and conduct ourselves as if we were citizens of another world. We are commanded to be in the world without being of it. There's this mystery about practical change that the worldly are unable to change the world. You can't change the world if you're completely worldly because then you're chained. So you have to have this ability to intuit, to envisage, to see beyond. This moment of defiance [is] related to the imagination, the second aspect of the mind, and that's the great humanizing task of poetry.

In this essay I want to put Kierkegaard, the nineteenth-century Danish philosopher, and Roberto Unger together with regards to the role of poetry. For Roberto Unger, poetry is a way to see beyond into the future; for Kierkegaard, the future is only a disposition to the past. It seems here that poets are then the Janus-faced writers. When I say *Janus-faced*, I am referring to Janus, the Roman god who is associated with doorways, beginnings, and transitions. Usually a two-faced god, he looks to both the future and the past at the same time. A Janus-faced writer is one way to think about being a poet. In the black diaspora by way of Ghana, particularly the Akan tribe, we call this ability to look into the past *Sankofa*.

> Sankofa . . . The literal translation of the word and the symbol is "it is not taboo to fetch what is at risk of being left behind." —Berea College | Carter G. Woodson Center

A poet in this respect could be called a *Sankofa writer*. This way of thinking is positioning a poet as a keeper of culture. It echoes Gwendolyn Brooks, who in Chicago in 1965 coined the term *verse journalism*, positioning the poet as a fly on the wall of society. The poets gathered in this anthology are keeping a record of modes of culture, particular ways of life that we can collectively talk about, change, develop, and grow.

One of my personal favorite definitions of poetry comes from *Merriam-Webster's Collegiate Dictionary*: "Writing that formulates a concentrated imaginative awareness of experience in language chosen and arranged to create a specific emotional response through meaning, sound, and rhythm."

"A concentrated imaginative awareness"—for me this means being alert to the things that are vivid and possible. Going again back to the imagination. All this ties into where we are about to go: surrealism.

SURREALISM: A SOCIETY WHERE EVERYONE WILL BE A POET

My favorite definition of a poet comes from an unlikely collective: the *Surrealists*. Who were the Surrealists? Why do I mention them in a collection of poetry?

The description of surrealism I love the most comes from, not surprisingly, one of my favorite poets, Suzanne Césaire. She described surrealism as "a movement emerging between the wars"; at the time, she was describing World War I and World War II in France.

Surrealism is an artistic movement that was begun in the 1920s by poet André Breton. A subversive movement by nature that has its roots in anti-colonial struggles, surrealism is framed by Robin D. G. Kelley in *Freedom Dreams*:

> What is surrealism? . . . Here is one answer from the Chicago Surrealist Group (1976):
>
> Surrealism is the exaltation of freedom, revolt, imagination and love. . . . [It] is above all a revolutionary movement. Its basic aim is to lessen and eventually to completely resolve the contradiction between everyday life and our wildest dreams. By definition subversive, surrealist thought and action are intended not only to discredit and destroy the forces of repression, but also to emancipate desire and supply it with new poetic weapons. . . . Beginning with the abolition of imaginative slavery, it advances to the creation of a free society in which everyone will be a poet—a society in which everyone will be able to develop his or her potentialities fully and freely.

When I think about *A Garden of Black Joy*, I think of surrealism. Surrealism is an invitation to decolonize the imagination in the name of the future. We will have to live together. To envision, in their words, "a free society in which everyone will be a poet"—to be clear, by *poet* they didn't only mean those who wrote poetry but those who are able to conceive of empathy and imagination. This is poetry as philosophy, as a kind of ontology. Poets as those who are committed to a kind of ethics. So what does it mean to imagine a society where everyone is a poet? For me this doesn't mean a society where every neighbor is submitting poems to the most popular journals, but more so a society where the impulse for public policy and the distribution of resources aren't market centered.

For example, when the Surrealists shout, "Disband the army and open the prisons!" what they are really saying is there has to be a more reasonable, health-centered, and humane way of holding people accountable than holding people in cages and fighting wars on behalf of a nationstate. When we are envisioning a poet in every home, a garden on every corner, and a movement outside every window, we are really thinking about two simple things: empathy and imagination. The prescriptions of these in everyday life make what we call here "the future" desirable.

FUTURE GARDENS: WHAT IF WE
BEGAN AT THE MARVELOUS?

On a personal note, I love the Surrealists because at the top of their agenda is a concept that doesn't get talked about enough: "the marvelous." The marvelous was defined as exacerbated beauty. Provoking a shudder in the reader or viewer. When I think about this collection, I am reminded that the location of the garden is also the location of the marvelous. A location of beautiful things. The question for Black Table Arts, the Because Black Life Conference, and all of us, really, is how these beautiful things will live together. The marvelous links us back to the fantastic. In the book I mentioned previously, *The Fantastic: A Structural Approach to a Literary Genre*, there are two ways readers and characters enter the Fantastic: through the uncanny and through the marvelous.

In that particular literary genre, the uncanny is a way to think about how to describe what happens after characters are presented questions of reality: *Is this real?* If there is a logical way to describe, for example, why someone thought they saw a ghost that wasn't intentional by way of spell or ritual (i.e., had too much to drink, bumped their head on a wall), then that experience is described as *uncanny*. However, if new laws of nature need to be created to respond to the experience of seeing a ghost, it is categorized as *the marvelous*.

When we enter *A Garden of Black Joy*, perhaps we enter the world of the marvelous. Perhaps in this world we are interested in the creation of new laws to live under. Laws that are interested in perpetuating and preserving a kind of ethics as opposed to perpetuating a kind of harm. What if laws were understood as collective commitments as opposed to modes of surveillance and policing? What might it mean to theorize around a location where the primary law is joy? How will that place be governed? Or will it be ungovernable?

In echo of Last Poets member Abiodun Oyewole, "We are suffering from a deficit of empathy and imagination." Surrealism and poetry have always gone hand in hand against the persisting wars and unjust laws to rescue us by way of play and adventure. If we are interested in recovering from a deficit of empathy and imagination, perhaps we are interested in increasing the quality of our sharing as a weapon against war and unjust law. How we share food, medicine, education, and shelter, to think of sharing as a programmatic orientation to community. A community without war.

This small anthology is interested in how we understand empathy not just as an emotion one can feel but as a constant activity of communities under constraints. Inside *A Garden of Black Joy*, we are thinking about how to put empathy not only on the ground but *in* the ground. Make it common sense that grows.

This book is one of the many projects Black Table Arts is trying to achieve, share, and use as a way to gather community in the public. You can call it a project in *growing* empathy. When I first got the idea for this book, a poetry anthology on black joy, I hoped it would gain interest and spread. It's humbling to know it reached as far and as wide as it did. For thirty days the call for submissions moved across borders internationally, which gets at the spirit of this book. Black mobility. This collection is rooted in a tradition of movement.

When I say black mobility, I am referring to small-scale examples of agency among black people to physically, artistically, mentally, and spiritually move out from under constraint toward other possibilities. This anthology is one example of these otherwise considerations in gathering.

Whether we are referring to Ashon T. Crawley's work in *Blackpentecostal Breath: The Aesthetics of Possibility*, looking at the black pentecostalism movement of the early twentieth century inside black churches and religious spaces that carved out time for black folks to shout and sweat, examining maroon communities of the antebellum South and Caribbean who gathered in swamps with their gardens to ward off militaries, or thinking of the Salons of the South that gathered black women to discuss the conditions of their lives, this anthology is an extension of temporal and spatial movement. An effort to gather while keeping our futures in mind.

Young people also moved this anthology forward. It's not a surprise, then, that our first submission for this project came from a young twelve-year-old poet in Chicago named Azariah Baker, who gives me hope for the future we are walking into. In her own words, her cover letter read:

My name is Azariah Baker. I am twelve years old, soon to be thirteen. I am an African American female. I live on the west side of Chicago. I believe that life isn't perfect but also that we shouldn't accept it. In my poems I hope to relate to people and normalize tricky topics that society has banished. I want people to know they are never alone. Even when it feels like it. Because there is power in numbers and labels. We are taught that labels are a slur but they are also a way of bringing us together, identifying, and knowing ourselves.

Azariah is on point. *I believe that life isn't perfect but also that we shouldn't accept it.* This gets at a very crucial element of what it means to be a poet again: imagination. The mental faculty that engages possibility. The ability to ask *What else is there?* or *What else could there be?* This idea of the imagination and *A Garden of Black Joy* also relates to descriptions we find in Richard Rorty's work *Philosophy as Poetry:*

We need to think of imagination not as the faculty that produces visual or auditory images but as a combination of novelty and luck. To be imaginative as opposed to merely being fantastical is to do something new and to be lucky enough to have that novelty be adopted by one's fellow humans.

I think Richard Rorty and Azariah would agree. Possibilities that can be adopted. I am interested in thinking about poetry as an artistic form that can get us to write, speak, and live out loud possibilities we offer up for adoption in everyday life and institutions.

Continuing with the theme of young people, one of my favorite dedications comes from Toni Cade Bambara. Born in Harlem, she is another seminal, foundational writer for me, who reimagined the short story, novel, and documentary film. She wrote a dedication to her mother in her novel *The Salt Eaters:*

> Mama, Helen Brent Henderson Cade Brehon, who in 1948, having come upon me daydreaming in the middle of the kitchen floor, mopped around me.

This dedication gets at a very important way we should approach young people, giving them time to create undistributed and unrestricted. This also ties to the work of Roberto Unger at Harvard Law, who I previously mentioned.

Roberto Unger is another important thinker, describing the role of education as to "recognize in each child a tongue-tied prophet." As guardians of tongue-tied prophets, the work of those featured in this anthology is to loosen the tongue. To give time to those who need time. If we want to create a better world, we need space to think through our ideas! To *mop around* young people as they sit on the kitchen floor seeding their imaginations with suggestions for the future.

BLACK FUGITIVITY INSIDE THE GARDEN: TO PLANT SEEDS AND RUN

Professor and scholar Imani Perry, speaking on a panel at Princeton University in October of 2016, said, "The moment we find ourselves in is one of capture." This is not only true but very important to reflect on. When we look at the American South, particularly the history of the antebellum plantation, we find that the greatest threat to black capture is black mobility.

Stephanie M. H. Camp describes the position of black mobility as a threat to the antebellum South plantation system in her groundbreaking book *Closer to Freedom: Enslaved Women and Everyday Resistance in the Plantation South*. She writes:

> Sallie Smith was like many other bond-women who, for short periods of time, occasionally ran away from overwork, violence, planter control, and the prying eyes of family and friends. Called "runways" by antebellum blacks and whites, and "truants" and "absentees" by historians, such women did not intend to make a break for freedom in the North but sought temporary escapes from oppressive regimes that compelled them to work as drudges for most of their lives and that intended to limit the time for and meaning of independent activity. (The words "runaway," "truant," and "absentee" are used here synonymously; "fugitive" refers to those who ran to the North.) For periods lasting a night, a week, or several weeks, enslaved women and men ran away to nearby woods, swamps, and the slave quarters of neighboring plantations.

> While planters dreamed and schemed about the creation of orderly plantations in which the location of enslaved people was neatly and determined by the laws, curfew, rules, and the demand of the crops, enslaved people engaged in truancy, a practice that distributed and in some cases alarmed slaveholders.

A Garden of Black Joy is interested in a space where absentees can gather and share. We are interested in the temporary escapes. Where truants and fugitives can laugh about important and unimportant things. Where collective projects can be programed. In almost all our community spaces, a topic that is inescapable is work. The conditions under which we perform our day jobs. This is particularly true in our Black Lines Matter writing program located at The Loft Literary Center. In these spaces we don't necessarily have suggestions on how to make these conditions better. Some of our conversations don't lead to offerings toward different employment. We don't suggest that an escape is permanent. What we do spotlight is *relatability*. What typically comes up is not only the fact that other members have worked under the same conditions but also reflections on how to get through the same conditions because we've all been there before. For our work, it is very important to know there are others living within the same conditions. This is also a kind of garden where beautiful things are.

This is a collection that is rooted at the edges. When we think about black experiments in living under constraints, it's at the edges that we find the garden. Particularly in maroon communities, temporal dwellings that dotted the American South and Caribbean. We find out more in the work of Richard Price's *Maroon Societies:*

> Making gardens was one of the first tasks for each newly formed maroon group; only one month after having established a new village, Yanga's people in Mexico "had already planted many seedlings and sugar cane and the vegetables" (Davidson 1966:247). And pursuing troops, fully understanding the maroons' dependence on their gardens, often made their destruction first order of business when attaching settlements.

This anthology thinks of joy as "a first task" to any "newly formed" gathering entangled with the maroon communities. Some of these poems play with the border and edge of the page, some don't acknowledge it altogether. Black experiments in living share in common with poetry, brevity. Brief emergences under constraints are a recurring happening of the black experience. Poetry, like black experiments in living, is often truncated, small, and brief. Nothing ever lasts too long.

Thinking of poetry as a kind of response to gardens and nature allows us to return to *the Fantastic.* Robert Scholes reminds us, "to justify its own existence, poetics must become a science," and to bring this into conversation with what Nick Pyenson tells us in *Spying On Whales,* "artists and scientists aren't so different when you consider how creative enterprises see the light of day." That poets and scientists eagerly observe and describe nature. One practitioner does it centering measurement, the other imagery and sensory detail.

The poets in this anthology bring their own descriptions of nature, their own worlds, and their own kitchens. They describe loved ones moping around them, relatives who are no longer with us, and the late-night orchestras of their communities. From Cape Town, South Africa, to Washington, DC, these writers have kept records of the sounds and textures of their lives.

I see this work gathered here as an experiment in living and mobility. In print we move. These poems called me to move. I write this in immense gratitude for those who made such a moment possible. We put the call out and the call was answered. Again and again. Over three hundred times. Inside and outside US territory, saying *Do you copy? Does this joy have a receiver?*

I am not sure if *A Garden of Black Joy* is a utopian space. I am leaning toward no. I think this collection of poetry holds the idea of Utopia in a complicated place. I agree with British urban fantasy author China Miéville as he describes a third form of place: *apocatopia*.

> Apocalypse and Utopia: the end of everything, and the horizon of hope. Far from antipodes, these two have always been inextricable . . . The one, the apocalypse, the end-times rending of the veil, paves the way for the other, the time beyond, the new beginning.

The end of everything and the horizon of hope. Some of these poems describe the end of everything. Some describe a horizon of hope. Most are a blend of both. In what is gathered here, the word "wound" can be a single sentence. These poems leave openings for the hurt and the heavy, but what is in each of them is language well exercised in possibility.

This anthology is a collection of poems that are trying to get us to think about how to become more capable of new things with others. Some provide instructions. These instructions might range from learning how to play dominoes to how to fry catfish. These poems cover ground. Empire has made a home in where we live; this anthology is interested in what might be possible in the cracks of its walls. In what we might call *the crevices of the concrete*.

So what does it mean to have an anthology dedicated to black joy in this stage of America? I believe as the Chicago Artists Coalition suggests— it means we are in a state of emergency and also a state of emergence.

A GOVERNMENT OF GARDENS: WHEN POETS WRITE THE LAW, WHAT DO THE CITIES SOUND LIKE?

If we begin at the marvelous—a location where gardens grow—and follow the path in front of us, we will eventually arrive in front of a government building greeted by two poets—Aimé Césaire and Léopold Sédar Senghor. These poet-politicians took up particular weapons to declare war against colonialism in the 1930s. Their weapons of choice were poetry and the Négritude movement.

The Négritude movement could be described as a long love letter of literature to Africa to raise black consciousness across the diaspora and to envision a postcolonial world.

This section being titled When Poets Write the Law is interesting considering Césaire actually has a history of refusing unjust laws—particularly around his 2005 refusal, at age 92, to meet with then-president of France Nicolas Sarkozy—because of a law "emphasizing the positive legacy of French colonialism."

Césaire saying he did not want "to appear to support the spirit and the letter of the law of 23rd February." Aimé Césaire and Léopold Sédar Senghor were poets at heart. Césaire serving as mayor of his homeland Martinique and Senghor serving as the first president of Senegal.

We should also think of my own city and the work of city council member and poet Andrea Jenkins, author of *The T Is Not Silent*. US Representative Keith Ellison described the work of Jenkins: "During her twelve-year career as policy aide for the Minneapolis City Council, Ms. Jenkins was central in raising the profile of transgender issues among Minnesota's most influential policy makers."

Perhaps inside *A Garden of Black Joy* we follow the lead of Aimé Césaire and refuse any law that tries to write as "good" the legacy of colonialism. Inside this garden, we echo Léopold Sédar Senghor, who, as described by the *New York Times*, "at the United Nations in 1961 [. . .] noted the double standards applied by some nations newly rid of colonialism. 'We have denounced the imperialism of the great powers only to secrete a miniature imperialism toward our neighbors.'"

A Garden of Black Joy isn't a place of "miniature imperialism," more so a place of miniature marvels that need seeding. Ideas that—as the surrealists would say—need new poetic weapons.

Inside *A Garden of Black Joy* we also follow the lead of Andrea Jenkins, who wrote in her poem "For One Who Tends To Gardens," "How do I protect this precious garden from the pests of life?" As response, this collection says "joy," defined here as a tilt toward being in relation with one another. In her poem "One time for yo mind," she says, "Why do we strive for the same ideals as the oppressor?"

Within the work of Aimé Césaire, Léopold Sédar Senghor, and Andrea Jenkins we see a sort of refusal and vision, with Césaire stating "I became a poet by renouncing poetry"—imagining and creating in spite of colonialism and what Césaire described as "thingification."

A question that could be raised from this collection is *What role can poetry play in imagining the future of a country?* I think a more important question could be *What role can poetry play in making "common sense" the requirements for community to continue?* Thinking through how shifting the question changes how we organize and what we create.

Places where poetry happens are some of the most interesting examples of democratic societies we have. We also have places in history we can look to for inspiration where poetry, democracy, and alternative economies meet. For example, Hangzhou, China. We can find more about this in *The Geography of Genius* by Eric Weiner; he elaborates:

> A poet-governor named Su Tungpo . . . Everyone in today's Hangzhou knows him and loves him . . . If block printing was the internet of its age, poetry was the Twitter. People communicated in short missives that packed a lot of meaning into only a few characters. Unlike in previous eras, when poetry was limited to divine subjects, Song era poetry, like today's social media, tackled every topic under the sun, from iron mines to body lice. In Hangzhou, as in Athens, the arts didn't stand apart from everyday life. It's difficult to underestimate the role that poetry played at the time. People could pay for wine and tea with copies of the most celebrated poems of the day. Regular competitions were held. Even children got involved.

Imperial China was also famous for its civil service examination system:

> These exams also involved poetry. People taking the exam were told to write out their arguments of what should be done in a given situation. The situations were often impossible, so there were no right answers; the goal was to see the complexity and to realize that something could be done to open up a situation for the better.

> In other parts of the exam, people were asked to write a poem. The test wasn't centered on whether you were a good poet. Instead, the person taking the exam could write a poem off the cuff that would affect the mood of the reader in the impossible situation being described.

Here we see poetry offering not only a mode of alternative economy but a way of organizing government power. More than a different example of economy and government, we see a reorientation of values. Art is considered a legitimate measure for leadership in government. It's also important to realize that these examples aren't ideal in any way and deserve to be looked at with suspicion.

The goal shouldn't be to use poetry to elect military officials or fill any position of power that involves violence or hierarchy. With this, however, there are plenty of questions that go unanswered, especially in terms of economy, considering who had access to copies of celebrated poems and what determined a celebrated poem rather than a noncelebrated poem. In light of these questions, I do think looking at history might open our imaginations and ignite new suggestions for where we're headed.

Perhaps this book could be a catalyst to emerge what Sheldon Wolin at Princeton University described as "Fugitive Democracy," as he understood democracy to be not a form of government but a moment in community. Again, we are reminded of the maroon communities and their experiments in fugitive democracy. Wolin writes:

> Democracy is not about where the political is located but how it is experienced. Revolutions activate the demos and destroy boundaries that bar access from political experience . . . Democracy thus seems destined to be a moment rather than a form. Throughout the history of political thought virtually all writers emphasize the unstable and temporary character of democracy . . . Why is its presence occasional and fugitive?

This anthology is interested in how poetry might serve as a precursor for these moments of fugitive democracy. At Black Table Arts we are interested in getting to the root of what is required for poetry to be heard in public—what we might call *a politics of regard*. Again, *democracy is not about where the political is located but how it is experienced*. What we are tasked with at Black Table Arts is shaping space for our community to have an experience, not only to give access to quality art and education but to *share* access to quality art and education. We mutually share with others—what I am calling here a politics of regard. We share access in a particular way to quality arts and political education, and our communities mutually share access to their lived experiences that make our programs and sharing possible. There is no us without them. It's very important not only that we know this but that we say it out loud. This is a different way of thinking about how moments of democracy are lived.

These spaces of regard constitute what is required for democracy to be fugitive because they help us understand the temporality of these moments and the capability communities have to always return to them. Poetry helps this happen. And yet we are full of trouble. Here, considering the work of China Miéville with our idea of *apocatopia*, I think Cedric Robinson will be useful. As he raises concern for the continuity of the Black Radical Tradition, he elaborates:

> If we are to move the Black Radical Tradition forward it is imperative that we understand it is not utopian. Rather it is about questing for freedom. It is about recognizing the importance of struggle regardless of outcomes. Nor does it begin or end intellectually.

These poems do not begin or end intellectually. They are simply a collection of gestures to consider otherwise. Finally and always to end on a note of surrealism. Especially to invoke the legacies of the Césaires, both Aimé Césaire and Suzanne Césaire, of whose work this anthology is a continued dispatch.

Perhaps this anthology is a new poetic weapon against what is described by Suzanne Césaire in "Discourse on Colonialism" as the "European printed page" that sought to eliminate and present as docile the cultural production of Africa. It strives to present a landscape of unbothered joy to which we dream new earths and new futures.

Further, my hope is that this anthology affirms the claim by W. E. B. Du Bois in *The Gift of Black Folk* that "the negro is primarily an artist." That black folk have "gained . . . [as] some slight compensation a sense of beauty, particularly for sound and color." "Herein lie buried many things," to echo how Du Bois greets us on the first page of *The Souls of Black Folk*. And yes, many things do lie buried in this garden.

Know that when you bury something in a garden, you are engaging in a practice of futurity. Growing takes time. This ecosystem and practice of futurity is also a mode of self-defense against erasure and capture because growing takes time. A garden on every corner. We move and grow in spite of. We are moving from (im)possibility to (in)possibility. Poetry is one way to make things happen. Many poets made this happen.

DEEP GRATITUDE: A THANK-YOU STILL GROWING

Thank you to Button Poetry, who helped us get the word out across the world. Thank you to my dear friend and colleague Jane Henderson, whose keen eye made all the difference editing this introduction. Thank you to another dear friend, Lisa Marie Brimmer, who suggested the connection to Wise Ink Creative Publishing for the project. Thank you to Dr. Joi Lewis, who facilitated that connection. Thank you to In Black Ink, who has been a treasure to the black writing community in Minnesota and helped us facilitate the community writing workshops. Thank you to Sherrie Williams and everyone at the Minnesota State Arts Board who saw the possibility in this garden. Thank you to the 388 poets from around the world who submitted. Thank you. Thank you. Thank you.

To close out, again let's return to the maroons. Consider this anthology a nod to those gardens. Consider what lies buried in these pages an extended response to those advancing enemy armies. Turn the pages slowly—you just might hear someone digging. Might see a poet planting a seed. In this garden we stumble, gain footing, and stumble again. We see as Suzanne Césaire saw "blocks of crystal stacked high," "infinite roads" in all directions.

Black Girl Artifacts

By Janel Cloyd

They gentrified pomegranates.
We used to call them chiny apples.
Twenty-five cents for big reds.
We peeled back the thick skins.
We chomped on the seeds
until they popped sweetness in our mouths.
Our greedy chins
dripped the red juice
on our good school clothes.
Every day after school
we commanded our place
on the skelly board court.
Stuffed our already
chewed gum in bottle tops,
watched them glide
into numbered squares.
We had Black girl precision.
Won so many times against the boys,
we would take their bottle tops as payment.
Those days,
the sun shined just for us.
We wore our Afro puffs proudly.
If we behaved,
our mamas would let
us wear a bang in our hair.
As long as at night,
we held it in place
with those pink sponge rollers
and fastened it
with a head scarf.

We were girly girls
with tomboy tendencies.
We kneeled down
in the Brooklyn dirt
to dig to China.
We knew with all our hearts
that we would get there.
So we digged.
And digged.
And digged.
We planted things that we wanted the
Chinese people to know about us.
We wanted someone to say,
we were good girls
worthy of remembering.

today i am not sober at the asylum chapel

By Adedayo Agarau

because the preacher wears white, & his tongue
beats against the wind with the memories of

clean water & mothers bathing their children
in symphonies beside a blue ocean   the waves
kicking their bruises away to places beyond their eyes

my mother's ghost is a palpable one
& in my pocket, i keep my father's shadow from falling

here at the asylum chapel   the preacher preaches about skin
says the wind slices through our soul says i am cities
found in one body—a metropolis courses through my veins

says black bodies have burned too much in earth
so my mother is in the chest of angels   says dead babies would

someday become funeral flowers   today at the asylum chapel
my mother walks into my room through the wall   brings
pictures of us laughing at the miracle growing from my palms

& purple-hearted men leading their children to light

Lillie Pearl Tells Joseph Bates Why *They* Need a New Five-Tier Mahogany Shelf

By Jermaine Thompson

And I won't say it's because I am the love
of your life who gave you better to do than sit
up on the porch at Big Boys', playing checkers,
gulping RC Colas, arguing about who the
Dodgers should call up first: Jackie or Satchel.

But, remember we framed that picture
of your grand-daddy from some years after
his freedom day. And that needs a place. We
just got the 8x10 from our Sunday at The Lake—
first time in twenty years the five daughters

could agree not to bring up how the sixth one left
her baby for us to raise while she high-tailed to Chicago
—the oldest grandbaby's Army portrait—the youngest
face-first into her birthday cake like a sow in new slop—
Didn't we laugh hard that day? Surely, those need a place.

I won't say it's because foxes have holes & birds have
nests, but Lillie Pearl has no place for her porcelain
roosters; no place for ceramic knickknacks & rummaged
whatnots; no place for the Bamileké vase Pastor brought
us back from Cameroon. Won't sass-mouth and point out

that like the promise of the Resurrection, Hemphill's Easter Blowout ·
will be over in three days. But, Joe—
                                        We have plowed, planted, &
picked. We have busheled & blanched & bagged.
We have pinched pennies & nibbled corners enough now
that we can afford a sip & a swallow from the plenty-cup.

This can be a totem to our pecan cheekbones, our wide-brimmed noses. A tower to time enough to smile—our moments, glad-ragged & jubileed, made into a monument, and Joe, there can never be enough monuments to family. And we can fit this one right back there in the pink room.

Ways of Pronouncing Rapper, 2017

By Daniel B. Summerhill

Lil Uzi Vert, MadeinTYO, Lil Yachty,

      how they make the tongue polysyllabic.
Stretching the way we wield our mouths to pronounce—

Musician

& an ecosystem
that sings our glory,
its grime and gospel.

What other way to sing autonomy?

What other way
      to sing,

than to break
our grammar
the way 808's shake
license plates loose
on the rears of big-body
American cars.

How we say,

A Boogie Wit da Hoodie,

& our minds retract all predictions
      and become bilingual
            three minutes at a time
as if to say
      we are unscripted

      —freestyle our names too.

Joy

By Melanie Henderson

sifts for black
in the blush of a summer lily,

the fat style in my upper chest,
breath given to sun,
out of light, lung plucking,
windless, spiraling,
a cork breaking cylinders
for berries, wine

if you knew, anther,
how strong the absence
of your skin,

touches, unsettles
pollen, sprinkled flour
in this yard, seeking to
properly break color,
mush petal & peduncle
into dye.

reasons why I prefer the Sims over anywhere you tryna be.

By dezireé a. brown

Here, I don't dream / of digging graves. I fall / in love with
a black woman who puts moons / in our shoes / as a prayer. No one
pickets / our wedding. Our neighbors don't ask how / we afford the
apricot / house or the pool / in the basement.

Here, there are no
police. / I don't carry / shovels in my pocket. I am a master
poet / that doesn't need to mummify the dead /

with words.
My wife and I adopt two black girls / that can't stop drawing pictures
of / themselves. They look in the mirror and see / Lupita. They aren't
afraid / of fireworks / and I allow water /

guns in the house. We
don't go / hungry. Here, we don't count our children / we don't know
how much / a child-sized plot / of land costs. My child does not wake
screaming / *Aiyana* with a lake /

in her throat. I renew / my vows with the same black woman / who
now takes the wind / into her mouth and tames it. Here, we raise /
daughters that breathe

underwater and soften
/ the sun. They are not buried beneath a bed of white / doves. Here,
they do not dream in chalk. / Here, I teach / them how to till / the
earth. Here, they don't hear / their names echoed /
in the dirt.

In Which My Body Is a Prize, and I Am the Winner

By Dominique "Mo" Durden

Ode to the stretch marks, and the belly button tucked away.
To the round face, and almond eyes.
The soft flesh with its own gravitational pull.
The scorched earth left behind.
A toast to the smooth skin, I call my own.
This is my body, take it and eat.
To bare legs.
To T-shirts and tank tops in the summer.
To growing roses from concrete.
To joy.

Joyful Joyful
(For Ms. Marjorie)

By Emiley Charley

From her parted lips
life excused itself in a whisper
and danced beyond us
into a light only seen
by the most precious of souls

Auntie would always say
"I'm Black.
Black like shadows in caves black
Like midnight woods in moonless zones black
Black berries
Black juice
Black juju in the evenings black.
And when I go, it is there that you will find me—
in that moment where light touches black,
and bleeds joy"

But I know she hasn't left
Spring is coming and I can already feel
her two step startin' under the trees

Miles in the Garden

By Latif Askia Ba

I find joy through the screen
of a white window
as my legs
like pendulums
swing and quiver,
toes pushing against lumber,
black elbows anchored,
burrowing into the sill

all to see a skinny pullo
with a large belly
listening to a dusty old
radio at the foot of
a lime wood garage
while he erects
a green garden fence.

As the sun beats down,
he sips his tonic and ginger.

Miles sounds better
with chimes
of ice cubes.

Walter

By Eric Lawing

Walter says he is Mississippi mud
bank
rich with the toil
of his ancestors—
his black?
his black is wind
imperceptible
to the light
that swings from it

When I asked Walter
if he believed in ghosts
he said: just look
at all that blood
in the damn water

look at how your body
is programmed to move
on another man's time

a ghost? is just a consequence
to an action
& *karma is a spirit*
employed by justice
understand?
(there are some things
unknown to simple skin
working full-time
in this universe)

Walter is unlike me;
he is upright and confident
in his illusion
he is a river that bends to the wave
of his own water

He speaks to ghosts even though
no one believes him

He tells me that they have
  a crown
   for him

I can't see it, but I believe
it's there   glowing   above
the apex of his skull
like a third eye

Wild Flowers: Octavia E. Butler, Roberto Unger, Ralph Waldo Emerson, and James H. Cone Walk into a Garden

By Keno Evol

A manual might make the point that one advantage to having a garden is that "there will be something to do." The garden, an oasis of bliss in comparison with arable fields where toil must rule, nevertheless contains weeds that have to be rooted out, and trees must be "reformed" by "good government."

—Yi-Fu Tuan,
Morality and Imagination: Paradoxes of Progress

The garden is the future. Where beautiful things are entangled. So let's imagine, if possible, a gathering. A series of activities. A network of procedures and programs that takes care of people. A network that is constantly taking new forms. A revolving atmosphere of local initiatives. Entangled with the state while dreaming of a world without one. This future place is a garden. Where we are now and also elsewhere. When I say *the garden is the future,* I am zeroing in on an example of plurality. A place where living things can thrive and flourish. What philosopher Ivan Illich describes as "conviviality."

The names incorporated into this title meet at the intersections of futurity and the public. Community and the commons. These thinkers have profoundly shaped my own organizing and the ways I think about service and the future. Each of these thinkers in their own way took their field of study by storm. When I say *storm,* I mean it in the way Roberto Unger uses the term—they took their discipline "in a direction it didn't intend to go," like storms take us, and pushed their field further or created an entirely new one.

Octavia E. Butler in the literary genre of science fiction, with her narratives of young black women as protagonists radically shaping and changing the world under high stakes and duress. Roberto Unger, with his theories of alternative futures in the field of philosophy, legal theory, and democratic thinking. James H. Cone, with his evidence that theology and black power are inextricably connected, particularly his work tackling the legacies of lynching and state-sanctioned violence in his 2011 book *The Cross and the Lynching Tree*, which I will reference later on. Ralph Waldo Emerson and Henry David Thoreau, with their school of thought *Transcendentalism* and its message that the divine is in nature and the collectivity of humanity; to that end, its goal to see the constructive genius of the everyday ordinary human being fulfilled and realized.

I would characterize each of these thinkers and writers not only as intellectuals but as prophets. Let me be clear—when I say prophets, I am not talking about people who perform miracles, occupy a place of purity, or even have a connection with a divine entity.

I am not talking about someone who even exists in a particular religious context. I am referring to prophets here, leaning again on the work of Unger, as "intellectuals of their time who were able to rescue humanity from a lack of imagination and love."

What I would like to do in the following pages is spotlight a few sections from their work and show how they laid an argument for futurity and cooperation in each of their particular vocabularies and vantage points. In this essay I am not suggesting that I am the first to put these writers together. I only want to add a few thoughts on what they might mean in helping us think about the future. My remarks are by no means an all-encompassing account of what these writers contributed or did. They are an attempt to pinpoint slivers of their thought as they relate to the future and cooperation.

I consider these thinkers wild insofar as their arguments had a relationship with the imagination and weren't bound to the dogma of their day. They contested the dominant direction of the nation-state or a field of study.

Perhaps a good place to begin is in the South, in the *garden* of James H. Cone. There you will find a tree and a church; James H. Cone perhaps walking in circles under a poplar tree, singing the blues on an Arkansas road. In his 2011 work *The Cross and the Lynching Tree,* Cone invites us to deepen insights into the connection between black social life, terror, and land, particularly the terror visited upon black people in the nineteenth and twentieth centuries by white Americans after the sunset of the Civil War, when federal troops were pulled from the south.

In *The Cross and the Lynching Tree*, Cone calls us to a site of possibility we can think of as a "garden" of black social life. A place of tension, resistance, pleasure, and bliss: the juke joint.

> Despite such terror, however, blacks did not let lynching completely squeeze the joy out of their lives. There was always a lot of excitement and joy at the juke joints, a people swinging with sexual passion on Friday and Saturday nights because then they could express themselves fully, let themselves go with no thought of tomorrow and the white man's disregard of their humanity.

I would like to connect James H. Cone's description of the juke joint to the work of Chinese American philosopher Yi-Fu Tuan, whom I quoted at the beginning of this piece. In his 1989 work *Morality and Imagination: Paradoxes of Progress*, he writes:

> The garden is not only a product of play but also an arena of play. Pictures of the Tudor garden show men and women playing cards, paddling in a stream, rolling on the ground, teasing monkeys, fishing in ponds, wandering about in a maze, chasing each other, making love . . . the serious world of work is left far behind in the pleasure garden.

I want to think of the juke joint as a kind of pleasure garden in the dark. A garden activated at midnight under its own governance. In *The Cross and the Lynching Tree*, we gain insight into the role of the blues in activating these midnight gardens. The Friday and Saturday night juke joint was not only an otherwise possibility in the South but a refusal and protest of the "hellhound" on the trail of black people. The pleasure garden of the juke joint was a different kind of invitation to be in trouble, insofar as I can imagine there were forms of duress there as well. However, this was a different kind of invitation in sharing. Inside the juke joint we see a choosing of trouble and the choosing of struggle under constraints chosen by those contained. People needed to get away. We see this garden spotlighted in the work of bluesmen Clarence Williams and Spencer Williams inside their song "The Royal Garden Blues."

> There goes that melody, it sounds so good to me,
> And I am up a tree,
> It's a shame, you don't know the name;
> It's a brand new blue,
> The Royal Garden Blues.

It's a shame, you don't know the name; It's a brand new blue. These lyrics were written during the Red Summer, a time period encompassing a series of terror attacks during the winter, spring, and summer of 1919 targeted at black populations over three dozen cities, resulting in hundreds of deaths across black communities. "Royal Garden Blues" shows us the location of the garden can also be the location of pain and ache. Places of bliss and brutality coexisting simultaneously is an inextricable theme of black experience. *There goes that melody, it sounds so good to me/ And I am up a tree.* The stark contrast is dizzying. If we return to the quote that began this piece—*the garden, an oasis of bliss in comparison with arable fields where toil must rule*—it seems the dichotomy between the garden and the field, bliss and turmoil, dissolves in "The Royal Garden Blues." Bliss and turmoil are entangled.

In Cone's work, a future is foreseeable under conditions of reckoning. We forfeit our future if white America can't come to terms with the practices of the two most dominant symbols in black social life: the cross and the lynching tree. How strange these two images, salvation and suffering. For Cone, white Americans cannot conceivably have a future clinging onto the contradiction of self-identifying as Christians and promoting and practicing crucifixion on black people. Cone writes:

> Until we can see the cross and the lynching tree together, until we can identify Christ with a "recrucified" black body hanging from a lynching tree, there can be no genuine understanding of Christian identity in America and no deliverance from the brutal legacy of slavery and white supremacy.

Considering this task, I am interested in being entangled with James H. Cone. When I refer to being *entangled*, I mean I have a series of questions. What if white America never comes to terms with this deep contradiction? What happens to black futures if that is the case? What happens to the future of white citizens? What descriptions do we have, right now, for that kind of living? Or even more crucial, how are we preparing for that kind of living? What happens to spaces like the juke joint? What happens to our pleasure gardens? I would like to deepen my entanglement with Cone's work. If it is the case that the majority of current citizens who were made to be white refuse to unlearn their whiteness in exchange for solidarity, are we to assume the future is uninhabitable? I am not suggesting Cone would say yes, I just don't hear a response. I think James H. Cone in this respect could be rescued by Octavia E. Butler.

Octavia E. Butler, who again, I would categorize as one of the leading prophets of the twentieth century, was a science fiction writer from Pasadena, California, who wrote between the late 1970s and the beginning of the twenty-first century. She meets us in a garden of a different kind. In Butler's work, the result of unreckoning has already uprooted America's infrastructure. Butler rescues James H. Cone by where she begins. For Butler, beginning inside uninhabitable futures is where we can continue to live.

There is still a story there. James is rescued by Butler. A prophet is rescued by a prophet. I don't want to suggest an antagonism between Butler and Cone, more so them holding hands within entanglement. There is a possible dialectical weeding that can take place in a garden where James H. Cone and Octavia Butler meet. Entanglement being defined as what Cone cites as *Hegelian dialectics* is "a contradiction of thesis and antithesis yielding to a creative synthesis." This is a rescuing of a different kind. We can see how Butler begins with uninhabitable futures with Came Manuel's description of Butler's *Parable of the Sower* in the book *The Day of Doom and the Memory of Slavery*:

> *Parable of the Sower* (1993) is Octavia Butler's apocalyptic vision of America and American society in the first two decades of the twenty-first century. The novel is written as a personal journal and each entry is introduced with excerpts from a spiritual book that the protagonist, Lauren Oya Olamina, published after the journal's events took place. The narrative is a passionate attack on the social ills of over industrialization and fierce competitiveness which have reduced a once prosperous country into a fractured society governed by outright violence and aggressiveness. It is a book about a historical dilemma which presents the image of a society laid waste, of human beings deprived of their humanity, and shows how the one-way journey of progress and mechanization has resulted in the demise of nature and even human life. America is presented as a dystopia with landscapes in which the hard edge of cruelty, violence, and domination is described in stark detail (Allison 472). . . . The possibilities of employment, material abundance, and an acceptable harmony of all citizens are gone.

Let's look at that again—*landscapes in which the hard edge of cruelty, violence, and domination is described in stark detail . . . and an acceptable harmony of all citizens are gone.* This is a different point of departure. Beginning within the bleak is a tug at the imagination. What should we do? What can we do? After the end of the world, when all conclusions have led to collapse, what will happen to the human being? Within *Parable of the Sower,* Lauren is a prophet, poet, and teenager tasked with living out loud the responses to those questions.

Cone and Butler in both their works position individuals as prophets. For Butler in *Parable of the Sower,* it is eighteen-year-old Lauren Oya Olamina, daughter of a Baptist preacher; for Cone in *The Cross and the Lynching Tree,* it is Martin Luther King Jr., son of a Baptist preacher. Both Lauren and Martin are tasked with organizing populations in a certain direction toward the future under duress and constraints inside America.

As it is well known and has been written about extensively, during the civil rights movement in the mid-1950s to the concluding years of the 1960s, King's tool and framework was principled nonviolence; for Lauren Oya Olamina, it's a belief system called Earthseed. Here we can see Martin Luther King Jr. and Lauren Oya Olamina rescue each other by being entangled with each other. Again a prophet rescues a prophet. They wouldn't have agreed on a host of issues, certainly not principled nonviolence. Lauren militantly defends herself numerous times through-out *Parable of the Sower* and the sequel *Parable of the Talents.*

I am also not sure how King would feel regarding a woman-led social and spiritual movement like Earthseed, given his own organization, the Southern Christian Leadership Conference (SCLC), fell short and did a disservice by not lifting up the leadership of black women—particularly the leadership of Ella Baker, who could precisely be called the Lauren Oya Olamina of the civil rights movement. To quote Julie Scelto in *Time* magazine:

> It was Baker who, first as an NAACP field secretary and later as its director of branches, spent the 1940s traveling from small town to small town, convincing ordinary black citizens—who had been enslaved and terrorized for more than 200 years—to join together and peaceably insist that they were deserving of basic human rights.

We also gain insight into the shortcomings of King in regards to his relationship with Baker inside professor/historian Barbara Ransby's seminal work *Ella Baker and the Black Freedom Movement:*

> Yet King kept Baker at arm's length and never treated her as a political or intellectual peer. As Baker later put it: "After all, who was I? I was female, I was old. I didn't have any Ph.D." Furthermore, she explained, she was "not loathe to raise questions. I did not just subscribe to a theory just because it came out of the mouth of the leader." She was not the kind of person that made special effort to be ingratiating. She was well aware, by the mid-1950s, that her forthrightness in the face of authority carried a certain price, limiting her acceptance by those in positions of official power, but it was a price she was willing to pay in order to think and act according to her conscience.

Ella Baker already had years of organizing under her belt by the time she traveled to Montgomery to help King start the groundwork for SCLC. It's so sad when prophets fail prophets. We lose prophetic possibility. Martin failed Ella. His falling into the shortcomings of sexism, misogynoir, and elitism with regards to who should lead is disappointing and historically frustrating. More could have been possible. However, there still seems to be some overlap once Martin Luther King and Octavia E. Butler walk into a garden together.

For Butler's protagonist Lauren, that garden is titled *ACORN*, a community she establishes by the end of *Parable of the Sower*; for Martin Luther King, it is the concept of *a beloved community*. These two gardens are entangled with each other, connected by theory and practice. King as theory; Lauren as practice and theory. In many ways, King's vision of a beloved community, particularly on the scale in which he envisioned, not only never happened in his lifetime but still has yet to be realized over fifty years later.

Dr. Martin Luther King Jr. was a religious leader and intellectual from Georgia who had a theory. He was more of a thinker than an organizer. He was more of an orator than someone with blueprints or a programmatic argument. He did have a very useful moral argument in a moment of American apartheid. He was a philosopher from the South who was courageous. He wasn't a veteran when the movement found him in the 1950s. Ella Baker was a veteran by the time King arrived on the scene. King's theory of a beloved community prophesied what America *could* become. And it didn't become that. Butler responds to the theory of King by way of Lauren saying *Here is what will happen when your theory isn't realized.* A preacher is rescued by a prophet.

That theory did, however, become what Octavia Butler wrote about in the 1990s. She got it right. In her follow-up *Parable of the Talents*, Butler writes of a fictional presidential candidate Andrew Jarret who "[has] no real platform, but he was charismatic and spoke to a frustrated American majority in an uncertain time with the slogan 'Make America Great Again.'" The election of Donald J. Trump in 2016 by way of his campaign slogan "Make America Great Again" is confirmation from Butler of the "I told you so" variety.

This is how Butler rescues King. She does so by describing a possibility beginning at the outer limits of King's imagination. Butler within her work did intellectual and imaginative work that the leading black men of the civil rights movement didn't do. Though perhaps here it is a good time to say, like the other thinkers I have discussed so far, I am also interested in being entangled with Octavia E. Butler, particularly with the concept of solutions. In a 1996 interview with Stephen W. Potts titled "We Keep Playing the Same Record," Butler speaks about her work, specifically her Parable series.

> **Stephen W. Potts:** I gather that we can expect another book to pick up where *Parable of the Sower* left off?
>
> **Octavia E. Butler:** Well, in *Parable of the Sower* I focused on the problems—the things we have done wrong, that appear we are doing wrong, and where those things can lead us. I made a real effort to talk about what could actually happen or is in the process of happening: the walled communities and the illiteracy and global warming and lots of other things. In *Parable of the Talents* I want to give my characters the chance to work on the solutions, to say "Here is the solution!"

I am interested here in being entangled with the concept of solutions. I am not suggesting solutions aren't real or important or that Octavia Butler thought she figured out a definitive solution in her work. I am also not suggesting that I disagree with small-scale belief systems empowering local communities to design better futures through high tech and philosophy. What I do want to do is think deeper about how we frame solutions. Particularly what a program for society needs in order to be valid or useful. In this respect I think Octavia E. Butler is entangled with

Brazilian philosopher and politician Roberto Mangabeira Unger. In an interview with *Big Think* in 2014 regarding social theory, Unger states:

So think of what happens today. If I propose something that is very distant from present reality you say *That's interesting, but it's utopian.* If I propose something that is close to what already exists you say *That's feasible, but it's trivial.* Thus everything that is proposed can be derided as either utopian or trivial. This false dilemma arises from a misunderstanding of the nature of the programmatic imagination. It's not about blueprints, it's about succession. It's not architecture—it's music.

For example, the task of rescuing . . . need not take the form of a comprehensive theory or philosophy. It can take the form of particular critical and explanatory practices . . . and once again in thought as in politics deep transformations can begin in small initiatives.

Butler and Unger would agree and disagree. For Butler's character Lauren in *Parable of the Talents*, the solution is to see Earthseed realized. A goal for Earthseed is to see humanity travel beyond the planet to cultivate civilization elsewhere. In Earthseed, god is change. Butler and Unger would most certainly agree that everything changes eventually. They would agree that nothing is outside of time, that time touches everything. Time allows things to change. Though I am not sure they would agree on Earthseed. Particularly looking to nature for a program to shape the future. In February 2019 in discussion with the *Blind Spots* series in London, Unger had this exchange with an audience member:

Roberto Unger: This is a characteristic quality of first world environmentalists. . . . History has disappointed us so we will now seek refuge in nature as a great garden. For a kind of post-structural, post-ideological politics where we will console ourselves from the bitter disappointment of historical experience.

Audience member: But do you think it's post-historical or just ignoring nature . . . is there nothing to believe from the wave that nature produces and regenerates and is abundant that can be mirrored in an economic system?

Roberto Unger: I will not join you in the veneration of nature. Nature has decreed my annihilation!

He could've been cranky that day.

Here I believe Octavia E. Butler and Roberto Unger are entangled. The garden Butler and Unger walk into is one of small initiatives where imagination grows. Imagination invites them to play together. Imagination is the entangling link. Imagination and experimentation. They are in love with the same point of departure. For them that point is the future. Lauren is an experimentalist who says like Unger that time is real. For Lauren, because time is real and time touches everything, we must take refuge in a belief system that uses nature as a conceptual framework to achieve human destiny. For Unger, no such frameworks will do. For Unger, because time is real we must experiment with *the others*. Human beings outside the single individual. Nature does not suffice; the "others" do. There are entanglements that I would like to have with Unger as well.

Roberto Unger not only took the fields of economics, philosophy, and legal theory by storm. He took them to war. In 2013, he said in an interview series titled *The Life and Work of Roberto Mangabeira Unger,* "Philosophy as we should conceive it today is the mind at war. Rebelling against all the constraints imposed on it by the established disciplines and predominant methods."

For Unger, human existence is shaped by three inevitable realities: life right now, alternative futures, and *the others*. Though this is quite perplexing because for as much talk as Unger disseminates into the others, he has not much to say about friendship. I don't know him personally. I am not sure if he has friends or not, though if you were to take his preoccupation with the others at face value, the others are of use insofar as they invite us to become bigger, to live a larger life—though he never gives the others names. He might occasionally reflect on immediate family, but friendship is not really unpacked in any particular memories in his project for transformation. A prophet is alone. He begins his Conduct of Life lecture at Harvard in 2019 by saying, "Well let's begin. This is our last class, sadly. As far as I am concerned it will go on forever. But I would be left alone."

I am interested in being entangled with Unger, particularly within the concept of the others. For Unger, the only way we transform society is by engagement with the others. The goal with the others is to be in the world but not of it. Unger's primary activity is to shake the structures of the dominant regimes through a series of interludes where along with the others, we resist, by which we become truly free. The interludes, however, never last long enough. The structures always return, almost as if they were mocking us. Nevertheless, we resist. For Unger, the human life is always infinite in relation to the structures, and the structures are always finite in relation to the human life. There is always more in the others than there can ever be in the structures. Through resisting with the others, we become bigger. The others are our salvation, but at the same time they also threaten us. They threaten us because we have to become vulnerable to them. We can only engage if we let down our shields. Every connection is a threat. Countless times a refrain in the thinking of Unger is "money transfers from the state are not a sufficient social cement"; only heightened vulnerability among equals will achieve the desired outcome, or in other words "love."

I want to push this idea further and deepen the entanglement of it. I am wondering what the quality of our relations is if we reduce the others, human beings outside the individual, down to their use toward a transformative project. What will be left of our time together? Or in other words, what will be left of our time in the garden if all we do is root out weeds and reform trees? I am not saying transformation isn't important. I am only asking, who is keeping track of time? The time we have together.

What if the others aren't a means to an end but an experience within themselves? John Keats says, "Man should not dispute or assert but whisper results to his neighbor . . . every human being might become great . . . and instead of democracy being a wide heath of furs and briers . . . here and there a remote pine or oak will become a great democracy of forest trees."

A garden of black joy is a garden insofar as it is a place where we can whisper with the others. Sure, we might whisper about transformative projects, or we might whisper about the garden. Roberto Unger is a romantic insofar as he is preoccupied with the possibility of engaging the others; I, however, would like to hear the names of his friends. In this respect I feel Unger can be rescued by Ralph Waldo Emerson. A prophet is rescued by friendship.

The garden Roberto Unger and Ralph Waldo Emerson walk into is one where vulnerability grows. Emerson, the Massachusetts lecturer who befriended a young Henry David Thoreau, had much to say about nature, transcendentalism, and the experience friendship held within itself.

Emerson says of friendship, "A friend is Janus-faced; he looks to the past and the future. He is a child of all my forgoing hours, the prophet of those to come, and the harbinger of a greater friend." This concept of the others we hear so frequently in the philosophy of Roberto Unger can't only be detached individuals that we will inevitably encounter by living. Continuing, Emerson says, "He who offers himself a candidate for that covenant comes up, like an Olympian, to the great games, where the first-born of the world are the competitors. He proposes himself for contests where Time, Want, Danger, are on the lists."

I am interested in a concrete conception of friendship. Comrades aren't abstract; friendships shouldn't be either. James Baldwin says of his friendship with Lorraine Hansberry in *Looking for Lorraine: The Radiant and Radical Life of Lorraine Hansberry* (written by Imani Perry), "There is a certain respect you have for those who you find on the same side of the barricades . . . listening to the accumulation of hooves and the advancing tanks." We should say the names of our friends out loud. Thoreau continues, "A name pronounced is the recognition of the individual to whom it belongs." Roberto Unger and Ralph Waldo Emerson are entangled.

Emerson always acknowledges the others by name. In *Solid Seasons: The Friendship of Henry David Thoreau and Ralph Waldo Emerson*, Jeffrey Carmer records how Emerson at age seventy-five, his memory failing, thought of Henry David Thoreau and called one afternoon to his wife Lidian, "What was the name of my best friend?"

Anyone who has read the work of Unger can see the profound influence Emerson has had on him; their vocabularies, if not almost identical, mirror each other. Roberto Unger says in an interview with Krista Tippett I referenced earlier in this book, "The question is—what conception on how to live, what Emerson called *the conduct of life*—goes together with this vision of institutional change . . . it begins with a puzzle . . . with all these revolutionary projects that have shaken up humanity for two hundred years, we have no developed credible image of how to live."

For Unger, we become more fully human by becoming more godlike not in the sense of omnipotence or having unlimited power but in our capability of transcendence and always being able to create more collectively. Emerson and Unger meet in a garden of shared vocabulary and philosophy. They both go toward the direction of divinity in their activities of a higher human life. Always upward. For Unger and Emerson we are only capable of going upward with the others, though for Emerson we know the names of whom he refers to as we ascend.

You can imagine the garden Unger and Emerson walk into being located in the backyard of a giant cathedral, though they never enter the building. For Unger, religion is not of use if it doesn't come to terms with irreparable flaws in the human condition, which for him are mortality, insatiability, and our susceptibility to belittlement; if you were to ask Unger, most religions do not come to terms with these. Emerson, a descendant of a long line of preachers, left the church already ordained after the death of his first wife Ellen—feeling unsatisfied with New England orthodoxy. Nevertheless, their vocabulary is undoubtedly rooted in Christian vernacular and frameworks. "In Genesis God himself strolls in the garden, in the cool evening," says Yi-Fu Tuan in the book I quoted at the start of this essay. The garden of Emerson and Unger is entangled with the others.

For me, if the garden is the future, it will be where "the others" are. The others who will explicitly be our friends before they will explicitly be our comrades. Through friendship they will take us by storm, which will inevitably take us in a direction we didn't intend to go, and it's in the storm of living that they will also become our prophets.

It is by living with others we come to realize we are the prophets we've been waiting for, ordinary folks, insofar as we make ourselves susceptible to being rescued by others. To be clear, as I'd hope I've been up until this point, I am not talking about divine saviors—I am talking about those who struggle alongside us. I am not talking about messiahs—I am talking about those with whom we are also shipwrecked. When we are rescued, we mutually share our imaginings and insights we have developed in our exile.

If prophets are intellectuals of their time who rescue humanity from a lack of imagination and love, then it makes sense why they don't usually build churches. They're too busy wandering the city telling other folks about power. I tried here to shed light on a few thinkers who wandered their cities telling other folks about power. They did so with great insight, courage, imagination, and vulnerability. All prophets at some point in their life put their hand on the wound of the untouchables, knowing they themselves belong to the class of untouchables—if they have not already been rendered untouchable by being with them. It's in our sharing that we touch our wounds. The future is ours to gather. So be wild, so you may live as if there were others in the garden.

Reverie: Satchmo in Oil

By Evelyn Burroughs

When the mud settles, a hefty
      bootblack Satchmo blares
at me through an iridescent
      gold trumpet from an oil
painting and in the background
      nameless, nimble fingers scale
"Clair de Lune" on an invisible
      keyboard and across the gallery

wall, another oil of Satchmo, a younger,
      leaner, yearning Louis Armstrong,
lost in deft finger-valve combinations
      of *When the saints go marching home*,
an alabaster loincloth drapes from
      his bronze and bruised horn,
raised from the treasured muddle
      of his blackness and mine.

Butter & Honey

By Evyan Roberts

Crawling all the way up, I match my back to the dark wood
of the headboard. And part the mountain of pillows

to make space for myself. Pillows on either side,
holding me in, like the bed could hug me this way.
Some days with my legs crossed, I'd

cup my hands over my knees, and flap my legs
like butterfly wings in anticipation.

Today, with my legs folded under me, I hold still,
eagerly sitting on my feet, waiting for my grandmother,

My feet covered with the faded yellow throw,
burrowing further under, inwards,
towards complete comfort. And

she's finally here. With tender warmth on a plate.
Bread, butter, and honey. Butter and honey on toast.
Honey and butter. Swirled together under the heat,

a cloudy glassy reflection. The sweet of the honey
meeting the creamy saltiness of the butter. And as I bite
deep, dropping crumbs in my lap, we listen to Brooklyn

streaming in with the breeze through the screenless window
while my fingers stick to each other as I eat.

Fuller Park Pool Days at 331 W. 45th St.

By Lester Batiste

Night runs with one of the slickest, hippest
and most supercilious out there. Minx
Stoops often wearing white with gilt rim
glasses and tooth. Stoops rolls round 47th St.
in his marshmallow nimbus, brushed waves
in back from Murray's hold. Gold chain dangling
red-bone wrangling, clouded teeth whose voice
is raspy deep—like Billy Dee.
He lived on 47th Street,
across the way from Fuller Park.

Night would always

stop in to see his friend, since Minx's garage
was a place for a light or a spark

before the pool locker-room or concrete cool.
Shining and whining because of the summertime heat,
Trees lean in to watch raisins dried up in the sun,

become revitalized shades of conquered

grapes with a splash of water.

During beet season, glocks sneeze when squeezed

and light the block like fireflies in the breeze.

On my knees,
not to pray or to get spanked, but rather

to receive instruction from Night Runner's shoulder motion—
as I stare at oak limbs kicking waves rippling chlorine and clear.
Near me
stands my little-big sister
above the water, but below the mahogany chief's
headdress of towels and Jet magazines.

In the shallows, Night signals her to jump!

In the deep, there are big kids

umber like me

dunking, jumping, and bumping cheerfully—

as the Chief's whistle blares warnings at them.
Outside the gate, a Southside pulsates and peeps.
In the shallows, Night roars, "C'mon lil mama,
you got to learn how to swim".

In my tearful eyes,

I know this is happiness.

The Adult Author from Her North Carolina Perch Speaks for Her Six-Year-Old Self

(After Rereading Alice Notley's "January")

By Grace C. Ocasio

The moon wants to take me on a tour of Vienna for my birthday,
lead me to a toy store where a gold package,
tall as a crape myrtle, awaits me,
my first name glittering red and blue in its center.

When I close my eyes, I see myself opening the package, a
life-sized porcelain doll falling out
like a wooden soldier Laurel and Hardy
left behind at the toy maker's shop.

If I had that package with me,
I'd make sure it stayed with me in fall and winter.
I'd ship it off to the Bering Strait in summer and spring.

Sometimes I get as close to the moon as I can. I
tickle it with my fingers.
Sometimes the moon looks like a Frisbee I can catch in my bare hands.
Sometimes I imagine I can twirl the moon in my hand,
that it shines like a stained-glass window.
Sometimes I want to bite into the moon, find it tastes like a peach.

Why is the moon parked in space?
Why doesn't it come down and live on earth?

The moon's a chandelier in space.
When it turns, it sounds like wind chimes.

Why doesn't the moon ever get lost?
Why doesn't it ever lose me?

If I could, I would dive under rocks to avoid the moon's glare. I
would dress up in leaves, from head to toe.
I wish the moon would shatter like a full-length mirror,
that its pieces would scatter across the plains
of Montana, Oklahoma, and Wyoming.

If the moon stops following me,
I will cartwheel all night on my front lawn.
I will pitch a tent in the darkest corner of my backyard
under a Japanese maple and chant a prayer
for the stars, let the night pour into my veins.

That Summer

By Guishard Revan

That summer,
sun rays tickled skin
and skin laughed
and blushed
a deeper tinge of brown.

A reminder,
that rain
is always
only temporary.

3am // A Sub-Altern Study

By Irene Vázquez

The night is blacker
than we are but not half as beautiful,
or nearly as free.
Kamau tells me there is no way of proving
I am not immortal
until I die, and here
in this room, this narrow
room, I believe him.

Zach puts on some music,
something bluesy
but with enough kick to dance to,
Prisca claps
out a beat, and our loving rings into the night
as we stand and stand
and keep standing, keep bopping, keep
rocking. With each snap, we inscribe
our names in the dictionary next to the entry
for joy.

We are here. We are named. We are buoyant.

We shape our own creation, crafting stories where
we live
in the present tense. Our God is Black, our God is good,
our God
has delivered us
into this moment, where our very hands become tuning forks for glad-
ness.
I spend the night laughing so hard I cry.

How beautiful, the ways we choose to overflow.

If it takes a village to raise a child,
then our children will have childhoods.
If it takes two million hands to change a lightbulb
then our lives will be full of light.

Since it takes countless deaths to show we are living,
we bury our dead, we remember their names, we
kiss them goodbye.

Here in this room where all are holy, all lives are made possible.
I disappear
into the rhythms of my mother and my grandmother before her,
I am subsumed
in a bevy of arms that will not let me go,
and I think about nothing.

//

If I say that God is real, that he saw me,
would you go with me? Call the future by my name before knowing
what it looks like?

If I love you, will you get up and go?

Hi Cotton

By Namir Fearce

Rooster croak at dawn
In the morning dew
woke to roux
bubblin' in pot
mama smile
granmama shot
a devil
in the toe for his fishing line
now all the granbabies fat n' fine
crooked letter-crooked letter I
I see a serpent coiled beneath the undergrow
resting fine
n' the nectarine
be still on the tree
plump on the vine
n' adam was turned to a bumble bee
the wind hum—sing gospel
tryna wooh us to sleep
But we funkin' to a house beat,
  funkin' to a house beat,
  funkin' to a house beat,
          beat

Rake the springtime across my sheets

By Ivy Irihamye

Rake the springtime across my sheets
Spill sweet honeysuckle nectar on my pillow
Call the hummingbirds back home
Spread sunlight, warm and rich
As coconut across my skin
Face tipped and palms facing up
For the calming and jolting touch of rain

Guide the summer into my shoulders
Let it blanket me with brisk heat
Humming its way down my back
Singing across my bare arms
And legs and face
It knows I am unused to being unprotected
And welcomes me kindly into its warmth

I am here

Negrotopia #3 (Self Portrait as Heaven)

By Julian Randall

> We like the promised land of the OGs.
> —Kanye West

Cue the Anthony Hamilton/and name me a mansion/tell everyone there
is space here/if you believe in the reincarnated/I am already somewhere/
that somebody has gone/ after they died/so I am heaven/cue the gold
clouds/the gospel songs/the voices you didn't know you missed/until you
heard them/for the first time/watch me glitter/ watch me gold/watch
me be exactly the show you were promised/forget what tried to kill you/
just for a second/forget its name/and only remember that it missed/cue
the wings/cue the rain/I promise this is not the end/I promise we get to
be everywhere now/I promise that
the only heaven/that can hold us/is us

A Wedding, or What We Unlearned from Descartes

By Kemi Alabi

Beloved, last night I doused us in good bourbon,
struck a match between our teeth, slid the lit head
lip to chest, throat zippered open and spilling.
Our union demands a sacrifice. Take my masks—
my wretched, immaculate children. Sharp smiles
bored by cavities. Braids thick with hair slashed off
lovers as they slept. The masks grew limbs and danced,
so last night, to the fire—plank pushed, cackling
as they bubbled and split. Then dreamless dark.
Then mercy, somehow, morning reached for me.
Sun found us swaddled in sweat-through sheets.
Gauze and salve while night wore off. O body,
always healing despite me. O body, twin spy
tasked against my plot to rush the dying,
guardian of the next world's sweets, yes,
I'll lick this salt. Yes, I'll wait our turn
because today, we hold hands, mother
each other, bathe in warm coconut oil.
Our union, our long baptism. O body,
all I forced you to know of thirst. Yes
body, you are owed a whole lake. Yes
body, I'll kiss our wrists, hold them
to our ears and spend our days
losing to the waves.

We Carry

after Niki Giovanni's "Cotton Candy on a Rainy Day"
and Lucille Clifton's "homage to my hips"

By Kateema Lee

To be born a girl and brown is to be born between joy
and bruise. Some of us learn to carry calm and grief
in name-brand bags and in tight crossways of cornrow;
some walk around with a don't mess with me smile;

some carry the blues passed down from sinners
and saints, small breaches in rhythm wearing
away mask after mask, losing beats between hits.
Some of us sing between bills, between babies,

between absence and loss, between wigs, loosening
threads and burned ends, between lovers of big butts
and the ones who praise everyone's *round hips* but ours.
Sometimes we are like worn nonstick surfaces; we burn

anything that touches unprotected seams. Some of us learn
that love, at times, is a fist waiting to find a place to plant,
and living can be *cotton candy on a rainy day*. We learn
to savor and save the sweet, to make sugary, melting threads
respites of joy, to dance as what's left washes away.

kinda free

By khaliah d. pitts

down came the rains and
made an ocean out of blank
porcelain. fill it

      then let the juices
      spill, over the folds and folds
      of your earth. monsoon

and flood the valley
between your breasts. watch them sway
in ripples you make

      the waves you create
      mold god from the wet air that
      licks your hairline and

brings your leaves back home
soil bound. soul bound for the
marinade. sit, wade

      in the stewing. let
      lavender get caught in the
      curls of your pubes. keep

the herbs close to the
gates and let you get heaven
high. feel slices of

      harvested suns, hot
      and bitter, biting ninnies
      rubbing scars out of

your soil, you tilled
and turned, loved then burned
just to see if thangs really

      grow from the ashes.
      you got this sis, lavender
      and lemon. you got

waters waters, wa-
ters and tears and tears and sweat
and jinn crawling from

      your skin. you got all
      the damn time for the soaking
      the marinating

the washing, the new
the cleansing, the baptism
the praying, the prayer

      the here, the now, the
      water, the tub, the hot, the
      release. releasing

the chains melting from your hairline
      and the sun bumping them breasts
and just in this moment, you have a moment to rest
      to be

to pretend you ain't gotta pay the water bill
      make believe you kinda free.

My Mama My Hood

By LaShawn Smith-Wright

My mama be a dangerous hood
That everyone has broken into
Fractured pavement the ghetto grow in
Be graffiti
And crack house
And weed man
That every addict searches for
To get that fix
Shake out those premature cries
And be held together by the seams of her flesh
Inhale the residual sickness of being away from her
My mama a nurturer everyone needs
Be a crime scene
Cop cars don't come to
Afraid her blackness might catch
Her hood not something they handled before
Her smile a happy they don't quite comprehend
The roots of her hair abandoned playgrounds
That I still make use of on a rainy day
That my body basks in
Urges to get close to
She be the kind of joy
You think is mythical
Be the magic
Black been searching for
Be better than chocolate
While on my period
My mama makes me constantly want to be on my period
Enjoy the sweetness of everything that is her
Have her at any time without judgement

Regardless of age
Or distance
Or anyone's opinion
I still need my mama
Still want to sit between her thighs
Encase my small body in between her dark endless flesh
Breathe in the cocoa butter permeating her skin
Retreat into her body and make it home
She be the project I keep finding myself trapped in
Be the only thing I search for
When I'm missing
She's not new to anyone but me
But she be every version of freedom we been searching for
Be blackness everyone borrowed from
Be Homeland
And Homeless
And Home
Be the strength everyone searches for in times of need
I'm always in need
Of my mama
For her black body
Holding mine
Making everything okay

Burning Inroads

By Maroula Blades

Summer is near; you're bound up by new perspectives on gender and racism.
You try to break down daily intrusions and microaggressions trained
to snag souls and deplete inner fires to miniscule blue sparks.
The sparks want to run headlong to singe a line written in cores:
God endows everyone with purpose from birth.
Since age six, *whiteness* came heavy-footed to sully my person.
A cohort of strength arose by deconstructing riddles like
what's behind the will of intrusions, executed by a dehumanizing gaze? And

can swarthy women & men still stand in a void left from centre following moonlight?
I waited, intuitive, let questions wade unburdened through senses.
Aches fought hard, gobbling light, writhing in motion; shook scared
to fall short of their goal, unable to steal shine from stars in dreams.
A sturdy wall stands around my sunflower garden, an orison of thanks:
Hearth radiates, contentment in the now of things; peace in being all I am.
Today, the *others* prevail, backs straight on a hillock of words: *Black lives matter!*
No longer will *black* voices succumb to vacuums following moonlight.

summer thoughts

By Lisa Marie Brimmer

i am twelve and running around
the building and oh your
tomboy legs just stretched
thin on the top of that swing's black
bar seat

why was i looking anyhow
my budding chest breathless
with august about to break
my thick rubbing thighs
making sugar

a crevasse of thoughts that always
fall off on you and off the hair
blonded by sun on the top of your
brown brown legs i hope one day
it becomes

clearer to me which came first
your legs or this thought this i
lonely and wondering
what's next

when i think about
what i do not
see i think about
my self

the underwater feeling
when you leave

the sink and
a lost ring

when i think about
what i do not see i think about
my mother

translated softly into
beginning my mother pressing
butter into flower
making pie cutting
the dough

when i think about
what i do not see

the boys
my age
them

naked chests packed high
tight by their clavicles the dirt
on them necks or their hands
picking tobacco

calling me girl too often
chewing their nail
beds raw

In the Morning

By Lauren Fields

This is a makeshift joy, crafted
in the breath between tears,
wrestled away from days that drain,

torn in the process, and sewn
with nothing stronger than satrap bones.
This joy is worn, but with its last shred

it tickles a shock into my diaphragm
and I laugh myself into a new
morning. Wake up, come and see
how we are both reborn.

Treasure

By May Livere

Did you bring the audio recorder? No, I forgot. Atmospheric cold, in that place where trees are glass. The fire burns out before it starts, to something that is soft on the skin. And true. Like the honey sold at the gate. Quick introductions to friendships that will last a lifetime. A prism of purple, cream, and orange at the front. They rename it Generosity Centre, and fill it with flowers, especially for the wanderer who needs a place to rest. Be quiet in the walkways, keep your phone on silent. Sisters of cloth, clean linen, and patent leather heels. There is a young mother in the hostel. She has come with her baby. What! Why? In this rain? Maybe the baby needs diapers, or a shawl . . . let's go and see her.

Don't throw stones into the well after you have quenched your thirst, he says. I remember many things, but mostly this one. And mother telling me to walk in her shadow when the sun was too hot.

At this very cold place, flowers are many and a policy pitch is necessary. Please do not pick the flowers, the signboard says. Tea is served at 5pm, tea and queen-cakes. When no one is looking we pocket a flask of tea, and gossip around it at night. About motherhood, and business ideas. We know we may never see each other again but this moment is ours. We are free to pick the flowers.

i learn time travel from Great Gramma Susie

By Ashley Davis

every night 9:30 sharp my Great Gramma
sends creaks down the spine of her N. Patton St stairwell
i catch her creep as i'm sprawled across the powder blue couch with a
shimmer of her gold tooth she tells me
"shuddup, im bout to eat me some ice-cream, sheeeiiittt"

draped in long white T-shirt, longer white panties
black durag with its tail waving
to the speed of her shuffling slippered feet
we giggle, loud enough my Gramma Fay calls from her bedroom "what's
got you girls makin all that noise downstairs!"

and SWOOSH! i watch my 95 year old Great Gramma turn 10
transport to her Gramma's living room with her baby sister
giggles tickling the flesh of their cheeks
sneaking sweets from somewhere
where the Georgia countryside

                              sun   the
                     did   as
            in   fast
       the   as
sky   moved

and church was everyday
and the heat was different
but the way she talked shit—
the same

the next day i walk into Gramma Fay's room
see her pink foam rollers lined up across her nightstand
and *SWISH!* i turn 8
wearing pink jellys and twisted plats snapped with sunflower barrettes
dipping curious fingers into perfumed creams swirled in avon bottles
on Grammas dresser

WHOOSH! i turn 11
standing next to my best friend who always smelt like baby oil
in a chaos apartment kitchen flooded with bubbles
spitting from the corners of a dishwasher we filled with dial soap
all we could do was laugh
cheeky giggles like Susie Mae and Annie Mae
at the bubbles, at each other, at the mess we made because damn
there is so much to learn

like, the gift of time travel is not the history it shows
it's the way a North Philly home can hold 50 years of spirit
in my Great Gramma's shuffle
to the freezer drawer with the klondike bars

it's the way i can sit at the window and watch this N. Patton street
for hours with Great Gramma Susie
dazing off to her harmonica hums
watch as she waves down Eric from up the block
a neighbor who calls her Gramma
to fix the front porch light, again
sweep up the dirt from the curb in front of her home

it's the way sitting with her is learning how to sit with myself
long enough to discover joy exists in my body
still enough to know what joy feels like

that it *t* i n g l e *s* across my shoulders and *bursts* in my chest

i'm still enough to name it
to point to it

joy.

h a p p e *n i* n g in my *b*od*y*

it's the way time travel teaches me how to listen, slow
like the sweat falling from a 1930s georgia country
10 year old forehead
who 85 years later
will still be singing
about sweets in the kitchen

How to Conjure the Sun

By Maya Angelique

My body is not a museum of horrors,

But a calabash of light and ancestral prayers.

When I dance,

My grandmothers join me.

They twirl me in soil, salt, and oil.

Douse me in whispering songs for perfume.

Sew me their secrets for a skirt.

Encourage my breasts to be free.

They lend me the wind as my mortar,

And they gave me my waist for a pestle.

As I move wildly in the dark,

I conjure the sun.

do you see it?

Maurisa Li-A-Ping

funeral homes uproot
and transform themselves
into schools and community centers

morgues and graveyards
plaster their grief
into skating rinks
and brooklyn backyard barbecues

flowers, of all shapes and sizes
yellow tulips, powder pink roses, lavender carnations
need not fear that someone's death will be their own

because here,

twelve foot flames sing a song of freedom
from prison rooftops, little cousins make it home to the block the sun
both rise and set on

ices beatbox on the back of black boys tongues
two teen lovers waltz to a cypher on 2-5th and saint nick
with laughter, that hangs off phone lines like sneakers

do you see it?
the day when all the black children live

An Ode to the Black Femmes' Group Chat

By Maya Williams

This is to my cousin sending us pics from Tinder
of a good-looking black dude she's seeing

      instead of another white dude messaging me
      on OkCupid to colonize my body

This is to my sister sending us a link of a funny-ass YouTube video

      instead of a well-meaning white person texting me
      about another dead body with their caption of "I'm sorry"

This is to my friend LaLa editing the pic from our night out
to assign us to a different character from *Living Single*

      instead of going to Twitter to see
      another overused *Friends* meme

To the "congratulations" for plans after graduation

To the "I'll reach out to her for you" for job searches

To the "You got dis gurrl" each time we feel like it's all too much

This is to the circle of virtual feedback to novel drafts
and poems that are more intentional than
any college English class workshop I can think of

This is to the open space to rant about
      white dudes' facial hair
      white dudes' skinny lips
      white dudes in general

This is to talking about the people who don't respond often
to the group chat, knowing damn well they can read everything
we're writing about them

This is to the digital space I'd choose over Black Twitter any day
(You heard me)

Thank you for making me smile each time I open my phone

Thank you for making the one thing I make sure my notifications
are on for

Memorial Day

By Derek D. Brown

I found a breach in the atrophy of my lungs
under the aging shade tree by my father's grave

The stoic hug of the low hanging branches
The pursed lips of the leaves in the wind
My dad blew wisdom from
beyond in the whispers of their rustle

There was a story there
One left behind for a fool
An impudent child, who thought being grown
meant knowing all things there is to be known
False

On those days when scratching the surface
masquerades as deep sea dive,
I often drown in the impossibility
of heart to hearts that will never know flesh

Today . . . was different
There was paternal banter in the breeze
Silver strands amongst the green grass on the roots
A comforting mosaic in the brittle of the bark

Today we talked
With no timbre of voice
or fist to bump
he still rapped to me with a hushed masculinity

Through musky sap

and swaying branches
my father gave me a word today
That word
was love

Twerking with Womanism on My Heart

By Mikey Cody Apollo

Title inspired by a Black woman's tweet

Blessed be what my mama gave me.
The hips that opened like wildflowers,
the seeds that run rampant while I gyrate
and twist
  and twist
       and twist.

Blessed be the way bodies move.
The way Black vibrates
like a surprised night sky,
      a concert hall,
       Milwaukee PrideFest,
the way Black jiggles
      in front of a laughing reflection.

Blessed be the evenings
where shame has no name.

When I am drunk off the energy,
off the vibes, the sweat,
  the sound of my own breath.

Matter of fact,

Blessed be the alcohol,
for it is, in fact, to blame.

Thank the tequila

for the confidence
the carefree burn
a story to tell
on a rainy day.

Blessed be me,
      in all of my glory,
  in this temple that
       twists and twists and twists.

Blessed be the Black girl body,
         and all that she is,
            in all she holds.

Picking Remains of a Song on a Body

By Mesioye Johnson

An orchestra pleats a body
into shape of things that go & might not come again,
I mean   things that stand in between
                    motion
                                        &   crumbs.
a woman's smiles kissed ashes,
forming romance bit by bit
at the edges of what turns us to a drowning paper—
 the same way we mould dreams into black,
free & flee & flee & free
(exactly how paper defines freedom in storm).
a room of recycling dirges sprouts
at the corner of my lips,
it opens like miracle
                    & dies   somewhere in my silence.
a silent city dies on a woman's body
& we could only shout *"close the window!"*
                            as if the body, an elastic wound
are hinges to this dark world,
            as if   we are mirrors to a wall holding fire,
                as if we reflect everything decreasing.
there is a place, my body, a dark museum
singeing me into histories.
at night, the moon colours my body with water
especially whenever I remember loss
& how
mother stretches it between her name.
I searched for a star in my body, at least
get a summary of what it is for the body

to be a cloud breeding rain &
all I see is a sea of scars,
who are you not to enjoy the coolness of what eats you up?
& every time I wish to hide my shadow,
I find my body as a missing dog
barking into a faraway forest.
& now, mother opens a book of my crumpled smiles,
a symmetry of certainty & errors,
& the wind echoing freedom
from a coffin flips her body,
& pleats my impossibility of being a word
in this book of lined illusions.
at least I still have a shape in what sweetens.
       A song lights a man.   Blackout.

Body Still Grows

By Millicent Campbell

I buried my body
Gave up this flesh
A seed bearing fruit with roots that run deep down in southern soil
Arms stretched wide underground
Birthing tree trunks with limbs strong enough to hold strange fruit
without weeping
Weeping willows
Head bowed down to worship
To hang low
And bow thy head
For the sun is out
Let us not offer our silence as sacrifice
Even the leaves rustle loud in this wind
When was the last time you thanked the dirt you came from
Dug your fingernails in ground colored melanin
Ground your knuckles into the womb that birthed you
If you dig deep enough you can still see grandma's hands
Beckoning you to come home with her left
Coaxing you to stay and live with her right
She writes new psalms on your palms every time they are open
This body broken
Perishing plant planted in black soil
Still grows

mini-fridge

(for cassandra, madeline, and joya)

By mia s. willis

i am the type that has a heart like a mini-fridge.

small; commercial function in compact space.
both cool and ice cold.

sometimes home to other people's leftovers.
sometimes home only to my own.

my heart freezer-burns the things that stay too long no matter how
badly i want to hold onto them.
keeps its contents fresh way past the printed expiration date.
won't let me throw out scraps that still feel salvageable.
like the prime rib i made her on new year's eve.
like the half of an omelette in the shape of her smile.
like the lone yoplait cup she promised to come back for but never did.

my heart has filaments that crave the next power surge.
is sometimes tougher than it looks and always tougher than it feels.
has a door that hangs crooked and lets vodka in with the pizza rolls.

my heart tucks the things it can't let go into its corners and waits for the
light to go out.
doesn't discriminate between handmade and store-bought.
has dents from all the places i've been and magnets from all the people
i've loved there.
usually takes a day or more to defrost completely.

my heart is a hand-me-down humming toward obsolescence.
a sign of my unwillingness to grow up.
completely unaware of its finite space.
always eager to protect new tupperware.
but best of all, my heart is full. full. full.

Musings for My Blue Boy

By Mekleit Dix

You've got hard hands.
Rough, tough, and heavy.
Skin the color of moonlight stretched tightly over tired knuckles.
They move so softly up my thighs,
with a timidness that makes me want to weep.
Instead, I laugh.
Shy. You're shy.
Ever grateful for the night that blankets your bones to hide the way your
cheeks heat,
you shrug.
  Who would have thought?
                    Certainly not that white woman who called me a—
I tuck my fingers under your shirt and press my palms against your hip
bones.
Anything to keep you from finishing that sentence.
              You know it's true at the end of the day, all I am to them is a—
For a second, I consider strangling you with your white, cotton shirt.
Pulled up over your face, I graciously muffle your recitement of the ugly
we witnessed earlier and the day before and last Tuesday and that one
time when we were at Whole Foods an—
Lovely purple lips crowned by prickly, black stubble pop out from under
the shirt collar
                              Cotton pickin', thuggin', Ni—
I lurch forward, wrap my fingers around your neck and kiss you over and
over and over an—
                              You know it's true.
Who's arguing with you?
Your palms feel warm from where I'm nestled between them.
But I love you here
I kiss each of your temples, and your flat button nose, the coarse curls

that flood over your widow's peak, onto your forehead, and I kiss your
chest. Once, twice, three times, and pray that only my lips meet your
skin here. Never bullets or closed coffins or the grate of being held
against the pavement.
Baby.

                                                                  Baby?
Soft and gentle. Lovely and mine.
I prop my chin up against your chest as you laugh at me. It's a sound
that tumbled out from deep in your bones and bubbles sweetly from
your lips. If only for a moment, here is our victory.
Moon shines, twinkling off our skin.

my daddy & 'nem

By Nicole Lawrence

taught me the bass beat of a stereo over bets &
a tray of dominoes be the holiest breaking of bread
cross any table. so every sabbath
right as the sun begins to set   i sit cross legged in my father's lap &
watch just before the horizon.
before me   a table framed by an array of men;
all black and gleaming with moonshined teeth dripping of laughter
and red stripe. their joy fresh enough to garnish a last meal.
hands pour out a tray. slick blocks of ivory—all speckled and split
into halves   like eulogies tumbling out across nailed wood
and i am reminded   that even death is all too familiar
like porcelain bathrooms
& black boys turned blue   over a dime.
watching from beneath them   a question. my eyes ask him,
how do you play with bone without falling apart?
a pile of aftermaths is split again by hands.   the sliding of a tile
answers,
it is not bone that holds the body together.
melanin can   be seized and   severed across an ocean
and still bind together
like laminin and
in a moment quicker than any match strike
these chains that never belonged can   shake   tremble and
fall for better bonds.
at a table in my uncle mikey's back porch
i look above me &   *my god*
i couldn't tell if it was the sun or joy that made him shine the way
he do
but my father

could light up a screened-door-cement-back-porch
faster than any match or footwork to beres hammond
feel good ever could
my daddy & 'nem—dred, mikey, & raff bright like a gleam
inna gyal pickney eye
taught me how after a sunset

                         the dark morning   still shine.

Benediction

By Nome Emeka Patrick

_____the hymn from St. Luke's chapel
_____wakes in my bones
_____*tantum ergo sacramentum…*
_____it is 5:30am. my demons fail
_____the umpteenth
___time
___moonlight walks away from my blind
_____heart alive, breath alive—
_____a prayer rephrased, resaid
_____come come rejoice with me
_____the conductor batons the choir
_____the priest meditates in his holiness
_____the pianist remembers paradise—
_____joy to the world
_____rejoice with me, souls rejoice
_____the first crow electrics the world
_____the alarm goes off: 6:00am
_____the birds retrieve their songs
_____my demons await another night
_____for now, the chapel wakes in my bones
_____*genitori, genitoque laus et iubilatio…*

Ode to the Pyre

By O'Phylia Smiley

I found my power
while dancing in the fire. The
black smoke cleansed my lungs.

Adopting Gardens as Experiments in Living and Black Resistance

Keno Evol Interviews Lisa Marie Brimmer

Keno Evol: I've been thinking a lot about this idea of *growing after*. After transitions, after mentors have passed away, and how we engage those transitions in our gardens and in our artistic practice. Considering this, perhaps a good place to start is to think and feel out loud about what gardening is doing for you as an artist in your work poetically or literally growing things out of the ground in the midst of or in spite of transitions.

Lisa Marie Brimmer: Yeah, for sure. So, for me gardening started to come into my life in 2012. I got an apartment with a beautiful, sunny patio and started to cultivate some plants and pots. There were so many herbs out there but it was mostly floral, mostly to beautify my space and to mostly enjoy some plant life.

Around the same time I was working with that garden, I got into a pretty horrible biking accident and someone smashed all the pots on my patio. This sense of destruction, chaos, and desertion was really alive for me as someone recovering from a traumatic brain injury at the time. And so that was a portal for me in a lot of ways.

In more recent years how I've come to the garden has been for this sense of enjoyment of the outdoors in urban spaces that can be hard to find even in Minneapolis that has so much green space. I live right off of downtown, which means I got to walk a little bit to get down there, which isn't as immediate, so I started growing a container garden, a more edible garden, a few years ago. In that time I started working with little tomatoes and peppers and they came up pretty decent. If you get a lot of those peppers you just want to eat them in everything you can put them in!

One thing I love about a garden is it does make you look at food in a different way. You're thinking *How can I use what I have?* You're not thinking *How can I get a bunch of stuff?* I feel like I went through a transition around being better about eating the vegetables I had in the fridge and caring for things in a different way because you have a different connection to how that food got to you.

We perhaps as a people have been thinking differently about that over the last five to ten years, acknowledging food justice movements have been going on much longer than that, but as we've been much more removed from subsistence-style living we can often forget how much toil can go into growing food.

You see it, you care for it, you're worried about when it gets too much water, you're worried about it when it doesn't get enough water, you're thinking about it if you want to go out of town because someone has to tend to it. Especially when you're working in a container garden setting because they get real sensitive with how much water they have. They don't have as much dirt to draw water from or spread water out to.

So I think a lot about that when working with container gardens. They're a little bit more delicate and a little bit more sensitive. Some of your victories are very strong and sometimes your losses hurt a little bit. You will watch things struggle out there.

Evol: So I am thinking about a lot, as always whenever you and me talk about anything. Particularly this idea of tending with the ultimate goal of watching growth and wondering how the practice of gardening connects to you as a transracial adoptee? Particularly thinking about in our homes were there conversations on blackness and land, especially if that land was a place for gardens?

Brimmer: So I grew up in a rural situation. I grew up south central Wisconsin, where gardens were regular and in common. The ability to walk down the street to Aunt Vie's house—not my Aunt Vie, but we definitely called her Aunt Vie. To go to her house and grab some ears of corn for dinner was a pretty frequent occurrence. I grew up in a situation where we had our own garden in our house, and then my paternal grandfather, grandmother, that lived down the street had a very large garden that they tried to cultivate. They lived a much more subsistence-style life; they were also Depression-era, so they had that sort of approach and relationship to gardening. For them a garden was about *How do we feed ourselves throughout the year?* I also grew up eating rabbit stew, so things like that that folks associate with a much more country upbringing. I giggle a little bit, but that's the reality.

So I didn't grow up with that as having a proximity to Blackness, but I suppose now as I am older I do see that more closely aligned. I do see also my maternal grandfather, this is my adopted kin, had a very large garden that was his entire backyard. He lived in Madison, Wisconsin, one of the bigger cities in Wisconsin. He was Italian American. They had this enormous garden. It was very intricate, it had a fountain!

Evol: Really?

Brimmer: Yes, honey! It had everything you could ever possibly want to eat in it! Melons, corn, squashes, beans, all herbs, multiple varieties of tomatoes, heavily cultivated and supported. Seed gathering. All of these things were a part of the conversations in this garden.

The ways in which I think that informs my understanding of a garden being a little bit of a sanctuary I think come into play there. As an adoptee, the way I look and talk about the garden, especially from a cultural perspective, is I look at Alice Walker's essay "In Search of Our Mothers' Garden" and the way she speaks of garden "as an opportunity to provide a screen of blooms against our memory of what is traumatic." For Walker, she is reflecting on her childhood growing up in poverty. And what she does in this essay is to speak to the Reconstruction era and the women who were growing up at that time. Toni Cade Bambara is also talking about what's available. The availability of different resources, in this case the availability of the smoke arts traditions, but also the availability of beautifying your garden space to cultivate a practice of being in relationship with the creativity that comes from being in a garden space. And that creativity being a balm to the difficulty of the past. And for me the garden is something I can focus on that helps me and supports me in finding a grounding and a relationship that is 1.) temporary as I find kinships to be, and 2.) immediate and fast as I find kinships to be.

So as an adoptee having been separated from cultural and familial ties and having to experience those losses plenty times over, because those are never complete. They are reviewed every time I am in conversation and I realize I don't have the same ties of kinship with my Black family or original family, however you want to put it.

That sense of loss is repeated and revisited many times in ways I think [situate] an adoptee in a certain way with refugee communities, with communities that have been dislocated from their land and deterritorialized, such as Indigenous communities. This cultural and familial loss is so highly palpable—it seems repaired to some degree by the ability to work with plant ancestors and to learn about how they are related and their medicinal qualities with the various aspects they carry.

I find this [is] all related to the work an adoptee can do in order to find a sense of home or repair. It's not necessarily about healing in that journey, though I think healing is a part of it. When you say healing, it sort of pathologizes an adoptee to say that they have something wrong with them.

Evol: Yes, exactly. So in regards to that, I am thinking about art as a way to share our narratives on our terms. Particularly I am thinking about the work of Chinese American philosopher Yi-Fu Tuan, who is mentioned elsewhere in this book as well. In his work *Morality and Imagination* he speaks on gardens, particularly how "in Greek and oriental thought they portray the garden as *haunted by muses* who inspire its visitors to poetry, philosophy and love." And I am wondering, do you think about these things in your garden? And to what extent does being in these spaces inform the shape and content of your artistic work?

Brimmer: So these last two years I've embarked on a much more intentional journey cultivating my own spiritual consciousness and my relationship to my ancestors. My relationship with the natural world and its medicinal qualities and really engaging in the garden in that way. One of the ways I see that manifested this year with my garden is that I did a lot more spell work. I was doing a lot more ritual. On the back porch, you know—some of the neighbors can see, some of them can't—either way working with a lot more blessing herbs and smoke and doing larger spells that weren't just private.

I am in this more public setting, outdoor setting, engaging with more earth, air, water in a way that's much more directly connected. Especially in this last year I've done more work into cultivating love spells on a much larger project level. This past June until now I was in one long ritual that I am actually going to close this afternoon, so it's interesting that we are talking about this today.

I was working with different herbs and flowers to think on a big level in terms of our heart space and where our hearts are at in this difficult time, especially under such a difficult administration. Particularly in the years after Black Lives Matter [was] happening under our Black president. How do we hold that and reconcile that while still finding the strength and the fortitude to move forward?

Toni Cade Bambara has this amazing quote that she said in conversation with Akasha Gloria Hull in a book, *Soul Talk*. She said, "What happens to people with active pineal glands under the leadership of deadheads?"

Evol: Deadheads? Wow.

Brimmer: Right! So I feel that has me thinking a lot about how we think and operate right now. Amazing folks like Graci Horne—she was at Standing Rock, and there are still water protectors at Standing Rock still being active. She was out there holding intergenerational space supporting community and doing intergenerational healing while creating new intertribal rituals. We are in an interesting time where this idea of new ritual—not necessarily new age—is super common.

We understand that we have some tools, that we are directly and indirectly related to those tools, and we are learning how to do those things without being appropriative. We are learning how to engage them in a respectful manner—a consent-based manner. Supporting some of these spiritual traditions and technologies that we do have access to. Because there are books out here like *Soul Talk* from Akasha Gloria Hull, there are books out here by Luisah Teish like *Jambalaya*, that are talking about how we incorporate under these difficult material conditions.

How do we get on? How do we survive? How do we maintain a level of spiritual consciousness in these moments of difficulty when we know our bodies and other bodies like ours are [experiencing] oppressions that are associated with ours? So I think it's interesting for us to be living and be able to talk about things in a way that's maybe unique and different than previous years.

Evol: Yeah, and I love that you brought up this current administration and the legalities that we are currently living under. Particularly I am wondering how landlords respond to gardens, because I know you've had some back and forth with that in your current living situation.

Brimmer: Oh, lord. Yeah, I think land use is a completely politicized experience for many folks living in city settings and I imagine actually in rural conditions [it is] as well. These land use requirements and regulations often tend to most heavily impact communities of color, particularly in the South where deterritorialization is literally taking place within African American communities that have been living on and owning land for years. We see that up here in gentrification, foreclosure . . . We also see that very locally in the various ways that certain land owners have values that promote a collective good, that understand that the beauty and functionality within the larger ecological system of one's land is important, so they're building Bee Gardens and establishing more common-use principles in how they organize and use their land. And then we see landlords that are careless in how they foster and steward their land.

I live on a plot that gets the right amount of sun where I could have a really gorgeous garden right on the corner of a highly pedestrian-centered area, and *what's not happening* is that being activated. *What's not happening* is the potential three days of work that it would take to weed anything away that is not of interest—to really spread a bunch of wild seed. There could be a lot of medicines that could be planted there we could use for everyone.

I am interested in the ways we talk about yard sign culture here in Minneapolis, where folks will have *All Are Welcomed Here* signs that are beautiful and colorful with [multiple] languages yet are not really interested in cultivating the types of change necessary that are so fucking easy. The kinds of change that is really easy to implement on a small-scale level within their own small spots of land. It can be small scale, it doesn't have to be large scale.

I just don't see a responsibility being taken on a neighborhood level for the public garden spaces that could be. I live in Whittier, and the ways it seems to be organized to me as a person with a master's-level education, [it seems I] should be able to use the internet in a way that is able to find things and make things accessible. I haven't been able to find a way to enter into community garden spaces in a way that wouldn't mean I would have to drive so far to do it. I haven't been able to find the points of entry. So that tells me something about the way that that system is organized. That there are politics at play even within this sort of idea of providing space for this kind of thing. While I know there are other neighborhoods in Minneapolis where it is much more accessible, it doesn't seem to be accessible to folks who are perhaps in the more densely populated neighborhoods in the city.

We already know that there are distinct differences between neighborhoods and what kinds of things folks have access to, but it's troubling to see that in such a diverse neighborhood such as Whittier.

Evol: Right, and that gets into this idea of sharing and our folks sharing what's in their gardens. I am wondering, do you ever invite friends over to your garden?

Brimmer: You know, it used to be a lot easier to invite friends over to hang out and garden and have a sip. I notice that this year a lot of people have mentioned how difficult this summer was or how bad it was, and I also noticed how infrequently people responded to invitations. And I think I am trying not to take it personally, and I don't think it is personal, I just think in a lot of ways we're struggling on how to remember how to share. We are struggling on finding the capacity within us to enter into more collaborative spaces because of how personally impacted we are by headlines that matter to us.

A part of the type of consciousness development that comes out of intersectional movements like Black Lives Matter is a wider understanding of how the oppressions of others affect us locally and globally, so it can be hard to get out of the headspace of emotional and spiritual disturbance that comes with that. We also live in a very technology-driven world—we are connected to social media in a way that feeds and fosters certain elements of that social relation that we need, but it also seems to be breeding other sorts of social anxiety.

There are certain levels of loneliness that I think are being experienced on a mass level that are beyond what many folks probably imagine.

Evol: Yes, absolutely, and to kind of close out here I would love to return to the garden and think about what are some recommendations you might give to someone—a seed, a plant, or a spell—who wants to see something beautiful grow that they can use? Particularly thinking about decolonization and the need to fortify our movements. What do we have to grow to lean toward more sustainable living and joy?

Brimmer: What's coming up strongest for me is mint.

Evol: Mint!

Brimmer: Mint! There are so many varieties of mint. It's very palliative, it's very stimulating, nurturing, and soothing. It stimulates our throat chakra and upper respiratory system and strengthens our ability to speak our inner truths. It's also more holistic to our third eye and our heart space. So that sort of soothing and instigating, agitating plant I believe is an important one to walk with. It's very hardy and easy to grow in certain ways. It has beautiful, deep roots that will wander, it requires to be put back—and you can cut it aggressively and it will get strong and bushy. You can just pluck some and pour hot water on it when you're done, you don't have to dry it. It doesn't have to be a production. It's pretty available. You can get it locally at a farmer's market and support a local economy. It's also not incredibly expensive; you can get a large bunch for two dollars, some-times less. I still haven't grown from seed, I'm not there yet.

I know my mint was the most resilient this summer even in light of a particular wet and cold growing season that we had. We did have those moments of heat, but it withstood all of those things.

baptist street social

By paul singleton iii

Maze featuring Frankie Beverly was the sound
    of Saturday nights over Sunnyside

where Mister Ware would be having folks
                over for drinks and he would
pull out his old vinyl copy of Happy Feelings

        to spread it all over our neighborhood
echoes from speakers would be climbing up hills

ii.

'twas Maze who lifted us up
out of that Valley

got us all up those hills

and over those big blue ridges
where we could fly high above

Beacon

"Beacon" originally appeared
in the Summer 2018 *Sixfold* issue.

By Olivia Dorsey Peacock

happiness was at the bottom
of an egg custard pie
where ferries sailed away

and to Beacon lights ice cream in hand
scuttling children leaping
thin brown bodies in thick coats on thick decks
to retreat to warm rooms
and sweets from father's dirty quarry hands
mother at the oven's edge
creasing lips into poised, anxious
unspoken passages and a voice into
a tickled clink.

uplifting the burdens that weigh us down

By Shavonna Walker

I've heard   before

that Black women
are the mules
of
the
world

and perhaps this is true

for I've never seen   anyone
carry   laughter
                                from

        one

                        continent

    to

        another

                the way we do

drink

By Tara Betts

"... I'm powerful with a little bit of tender."
—Janelle Monae

Brought on by just enough sweat,
the bright colors and shimmers
trapped in hair, nails, clothes,
skin, yes, glistening peacock
of melinated skin, hums.

The bullets and elegies dissolve
in our laughter while we create
the next origami while everyone
            wonders how such folds arise
from a flat sheet of paper.

When it unfolds, we will find
kisses unclenched like fists
gone soft. A brown sugar
liquefied on tongues frees
the parched mouth, as we

drink juice drawn from within.
We have all we needed.
Let the quenching begin.

Afro-Futurist Vignettes

By Taylor Scott

i.

in a mirror   a black girl

marvels her electric curl pattern   thinks

a black god struck me into creation.

ii.

relishing almost-summer   a black boy

walks down the street   knows full well

he is a flower worth blooming.

iii.

two black queer girls are

sweatingdancinghootinglost

at play   transported

their bodies   soliloquies

recited to the moon   tongues

are meant for kissing   tongues

find god in ungodly hours.

iv.

there is a black man at a piano

and for the first time

he doesn't know what to do with his hands

his knuckles sootblack against the worn keys

he woke and didn't have the blues   the blues

didn't bite him for breakfast nor

did she sit with him at the piano

his back a bass arced by baby cherubs.

v.

a mother is supine   rubbing her belly   drinking tea

dreaming all the things her brown baby will be.

The Wind Kissed Keisha

By Salaam Green

Baby fat cheeks
Bubble gum bubbles that touch the sky
Cotton soft puffs of air—music in between her teeth
Keisha smiles, widening of her lips announcing she is alive
Existing as sugar, Sunday morning syrup, and hot potato chips
            Baby fat cheeks
Banana *Laffy Taffys*, 50 cent dressed in icing cookies, Auntie's sunshine
birthday pound cake
Honey written on her tongue
A messy ring pop her first love
Soft fleshy palms slapping brave jaws into place
Sour candy triggering her to lose her religion
Swearing with her mouth closed
Begging the man behind the counter at the Chevron for a multi-
colored Crazy *Straw*
Quick as a southern cricket drinking a cold cherry pop
Fizzy bursts of laughter
Gushes of brown liquid escaping through her nose
Keisha belches floating in a gooey world
Forgetting to protect her new silver tight braces
        No damn sweets for God's sake Keisha, "Says her Mama."
        But the wind kissed my cheeks Mama, "Keisha proclaims!"
Whispering hymns that sound like butter
Cocoa dreams deliciously becoming breath
Coming over Keisha.

Super Bowl on Streamwood Drive

By Tayo Omisore

I never got why we called it *half & half*
if the gallon container of sweet tea mix

on its way to marry a slim pitcher of tender lemon,
eager to consummate,

only ventured out of its pantry twice before its inevitable grave.
They say something about summer gives everything a sweet tooth

and boy, did the summer make a meal out of us,
young leather skinned children slicking ourselves

sugar until sweat polished our skin
into dark, unsheathed swords.

This concrete field, our god given land,
every touchdown, a coronation.

A taste of what it was like
to own something.

We played football on a blacktop sized kingdom
the only time we'd see a pig fly past us

and believe in a future that would willingly home us.
In those days, none of our parents' watches were working,

maybe because they always were,
but we played on burning streets with the sun

baking in a june yellow, so shit maybe we got used to
a world on fire too soon but anyway

in those days, none of our parents' watches worked,
maybe because they too were always broke

so we played and played and played
until the dusk covered us a shade blacker

and the streetlights flicker-mooned themselves into a path back home
and we always had a home to go back to.

Up Close

By Quartez Harris

when the sun climbed into bed, black children
gutted swings from their local park,
    where chalk outlines
on the basketball
flooring had become three point lines.

    they scaled the brown body
of a low-income apartment,
stood on its head,
    hung swings around its neck
       & sat on them like birds perched on power wires.
  all of them united in hope of their
    black bodies being seen
by the world outside the red hazard tape
    that had surrounded their side of the city.

    nobody noticed all the names on their bodies,
so they climbed down the swings,
  gathered a fist full of small rocks,
ran like dirt bikes along the nearest overpass,
     threw the rocks at the white skin of cars,

     a prayer to be noticed
just as anyone of those rocks.

     a car abruptly dug its teeth into the road,
  someone stormed out.
their eyes met like knives
    brushing against each other.

those kids rejoiced like a flock
                    of maple leaves reunited in the gust of autumn winds
because, finally,
        somebody noticed them,
    despite a world
too afraid to see them up close.

Sleep

By Tumelo Cassandra Twala

To be queer is a sleep we are too accustomed to
There is no rainbow color in our vision
We dream not in images but in the sounds
Of our neighbors shouting in loud voices calling
Us to wear this sheep's clothing and follow a god
Whose rod parted no seas for us.
Made no room for us.
To be queer is African,
It is your blood mixing with the soil when they tell you that you are not
fit for this land,
Fit for this brown, A curse the ancestors have yet to deal with,
It is being the wind, the trees, the soil and the sun because
You've always been seen
as less than
human

.

To be queer is not a phase, but
It is the moon shedding every night
Saying that although she is not the sun you are accustomed to,
She is all shades of bright, all fractions of whole
A beam of dim light,
But is light regardless.
To be queer, is a sleep we are too accustomed to,
But when I wake up and your face is the first thing I see,
The first world I encounter, the first sign of a life besides me,
To be queer is right,
To be queer in love
Is joy.

of the white tee

By Jorrell Watkins

bruh, ain't a new
white tee the most
necessary dress to boom
a Black boy's joy? don't he—

look so fresh
and clean, his white tee
nearly kisses his knees, veiled
by his name-brand jeans which
saddles the heels of his air force ones.

ain't this gown
for him to stroll down the block:
        pass shorties rocking hoops
round their hips and ears,
        pass homies fixing a jay
and the laces of their jays,
        pass junkies sucking the
blues from a bottle or needle dry.

won't them folks
dazzled by his gleam,
        yo!
don't he almost glow
into an angel before
a sole streetlight
shines a halo out
of the basketball rim—

under which other
white tees will join him
in tossing the rock   once swung
between the archway of someone's legs
then flung from half-court
by a tee, who's too short
to play center but has a jumper
that makes the whole
backboard thunder—

don't their bird's chests swell
for a moment of breathlessness
          feeling free in their white tees from:
the anxiety of a troubled city,
the flash of a badge,
the leer behind the wheel,
the description that matches them all

          these boys flock away as doves
at the burst of noise that sounds
like anything but their joy.

Flipping a Table to End a Game of Spades Means I Love You

By Quintin Collins

When God set fire to Sodom and Gomorrah, he rolled his wrist
      in the same way, the revolution and flick flinging wrath
with a *thwack*. It sounds like skin slapping skin, making the victim
      a pillar of salt as the big joker smacks the tabletop.

This full-body-get-up-from-your-seat smackdown in spades
      was prophesied in the smack talk before the game started, the
dealer shuffling cards with a flutter like your auntie floating
      about the backyard to Frankie Beverly. The cookout cools

down to uncles cradling one beer too many and slices of 7-Up cake.
      Little cousins sugar-swollen but sleepy bounce, giggle
as the first kings collect books. *Renigga* accusations cut the card
      game with yelling—unsuited for someone's mama's house.

So the chatter chills, crickets calling the sun down behind the trees,
      citronella torches foretelling the fire to descend on the cards.
When it comes, a queen to beat, all kings and aces accounted,
      a cocked elbow goes forth, rising to meet mosquitos flitting

in search of fresh blood. That joker makes James Brown scream
      on the stereo. Somebody down from aggravation
with God or bad luck, the table lifts. All cards cascade on concrete.
      Don't recount the books. Just run it back, elbow, wrist ready.

keep on survivin'

By Patience Imolele

at midnight we pour
pink lemonade into
small plastic cups,
blow up balloons to
fill the lounge

when mum laughs
she throws her whole body
forward, spilling drink
out of her nose

sometimes
we watch the news
to learn what
we already know

ava teaches me the
lyrics to survivor

every day is a
victory

This Must Be the Place (Or, Walking Home, I am Reminded to Buy Champagne and Overalls)

By Alexus Erin

1.

I was cooking to make house home
and wearing dark green, floating Grafton Street
phantasmic, buying flowers to top all the Thanksgiving dishes.
It stalked,
dressed in suede and maroon—I hardly ever thought to run.
In fact, I forgot the captivity for weeks on end
(This makes sense, busy is busy,

and we're busy people: when Maya Angelou passed,
we just pretended she hadn't
Willed the harried solemn to be evidence of standard protocol—
the room held no new weight. No time
to mourn
To consider our own liberation, as she would have wanted.
Smoothing spread on the crackers, we ignored the fissures
their rough-ground salt grains made on the spackled layer) The nightmare
before the nightmare:
It made habit of asking, night after night, if I was afraid
Pressing boundaries, granted their existence, on anything venial. Its breathing,
mixed with the sound of the radiator
Talk,
Radiator.

It attended the oven, sprinkling petals in all the food, as I had requested,
sneery and splitting the baked macaroni

between with-peas and without; dragging a jagged line through the mush
in the glass dish, borrowed from who knows where
with a spoon I had never seen before,
but with it,
I soon became familiar

2.

I cannot guarantee
these are comparable in natural light.
It, still, isn't easy for me: I watched myself

clean the bad jokes off the stove after dinner. Which is to say,
I cleaned extortion from the stove
after dinner
Often out-of-body

The stove, itself, maybe thinking
"they endured"
Like family can
To save itself, I mean

To outdo the familiar
To build a reference point
Better, sometimes,

there were days I lived with strangers. We only knew three chords
To riff apart the quiet
Medley every song we knew could fit
A lengthening afternoon, waiting to sing, free:
"When you walk in the room, I see things that I can't understand
I want you endlessly,"

3.

A word on home:

There is my mother, definitely overdoing it with the sugar cane
Bunched and bought, crowding the counter
of a childhood, one and only
Roots, shoots, a bag of ginger Joint junctures thready, akimbo

Home, a codeword for
our school bus stopped in the rain
Beckoning the geese, we are lit up inside from the floodlight. This new
ontological positioning:
late for school, thus defying natural order, traffic, time

or, 1999—
crawling, confident, toward Naomi Shihab Nye,
who sat in a chair in the middle of the sea-coloured carpet, reading
poems aloud
in the Lower School music room
where I loved to listen to songs about God: testimony echolocating
an early signal to persevere
In Christ: a new creation. Which is to say, with grace

wash, rinse, repeat
Good method into ritual
Ritual to method, learned more

cure, or,
It is certainly enough
for today: willing only one thing

To transcend the comforts of the state—this must be the place
To sleep, to work, to celebrate

Lyric featured is from "When You Walk in the Room" by Fyfe Dangerfield

joy (at the curve of my son's dimple)

By Ricardo Lowe Jr.

at the curve
of my son's dimple,
i find joy.
it glides along the arch
of his brown smile.
then becomes a
rose in his
cheek.

i pull him
close to my chest.
and feel my heart
blush.
i plant a kiss
on his princely crown.
and feel my eyes
water.

this little brown boy
wears glory in
his face.
i dig into his dimple for joy
before soldiering into
this wintry hell we call america.

nebula

By Salisa Grant

god placed one thousand galaxies between your two front teeth,
breathe,
exhale and ignite this city.
you,
are a living memory of play fights and fleeting moonlight.

of journeys north, then south
as each fluorescent footfall fostered flowers,
filled forests.

here, unwrap
a sandbox world, unprepared for your size,
for your dimpled brown thighs
your pull
with the sunrise.

smile,
and spray a love written in permanence across three counties.

dance,
raising clammy hands,
mahogany body spilling divine from distressed shorts and tops you cropped.
body yours, yours, yours
sweat yours
voice yours
name yours.

you,
a euphoric fog
a *real black* night sky.

you,
too much for *small petty places*
you,
hard to pronounce
etched lightly into door jams and handles
when and where you enter.

you,
making them work, for your gaze.

you,
galaxy girl
you,
crochet braids swinging
you,
muddy middle fingers at the ready.

you,
a firestorm of laughter,
you are the now, the then, the hereafter.

Tear

By Praise Flowers

a
piece
of soul from
our empire. Leave
their remains scattered
on the rickety doorsteps of
the church. Then, tell us that
our dark bodies are a reprobate
sanctuary. Make sure not to dirty
the pedestal on which you stand,
with the blood of our fellow man.
Remind us that we are the cat-
alyst for strife. Indict us w-
hen our bones drop.

The Elusive Joy of Elevation

By Victor A. Kwansa

Shooting hoops
Because you're enthralled
By the seemingly permanent spin of the ball,
Not because you think it's probably
Your only way of overturning
Never-ending cycles of poverty.

Holding a hand up
After the ball leaves your fingertips
Because it helps you orchestrate
The "swish" of the net,
Not because you're trying
To convince the police
That you're not a threat.

And jumping high in the air
For a 360-degree dunk
Because you can,
Not because your ability to do so
In a manner that's crowd-pleasing
May determine whether the masses wrap their heads around the fact
That you're a human being.

Strategies

By Valérie Déus

your picture from the park
made me blush
transforming me from
dusk to tobacco
in one sip
one word in and I knew
we were holding each other
somewhere in the blue

In this revolution
I think you have
my mother's hair
roller waves back to
the Black future
with a defiant bounce

I sit and thank you with my hand
in a way both real and imagined

you're the type
of alchemy that
works on me

Ask me again about sleep
when your face is a grainy shadow
of shivering grey dots
In the middle of the night
are you waiting for something?

Siren

By Simone-Marie Feigenbaum

"Black girls can't be mermaids."
I'm not.
I'm a siren: sing songs to drag sailors down
into depths where they buried my ancestors, rip flesh
from bones with whip sharp fangs. I am
my ancestors' wildest dreams. I am
the monster you dream in the dark.
I am.

they thought water and didn't think to think of us

By Brittany Marshall

They didn't think our bodies would make it out/of the water/
because too much of anything can kill any   body except this/
           body/   filled/with so much surety/ the
water begged for our forgiveness   and we don't mind
stepping out/   of ourselves/to conceive   of   ourselves/
we'll delight in the storm/and we'll rejoice in its carnage/because in
the morning/they'll wake up/with our scents/wafting from their
rubbish.

A storm/is all about perspective/   and there are many
names for joy/   woman/woman*ed*/wonder/water/wind/womb/
they didn't think we could embody all of them at once and what is
joy/   but the aftermath of a storm/where the world has to
watch the havoc/wrecked onto our bodies/and see the lull/
we can leave behind.

They thought water/and didn't think/   to think of us/but i/
think of water/and think of the way it clings to my body/how i
sometimes wish it was forever/how i remember it actually can be/
because tonight/
we'll rejoice in yemaya/and candle our way back to the ocean/out of
sight/out of
mind/and out of
harm's
                                                        way/

Children of Lesser Gods

By Wálé Àyìnlá

I teach my students government
—how to run a state. They think

joy is a state of emergency &
the constitution is a shadow of grief.

Suppose the boy I am tethers light
to the sun & I get to live in a room

of flowers & happiness bounces back
into the body at the other side

of the mirror. Suppose I find my voice
in the dance steps of a pen on paper.

& I stare at heaven knowing
there's a place waiting for angels.

Alone in the mirror, I peel sadness
off my skin in replacement for a giggle.

The sun shares in the laughter, spreading
its hands over my face to my chest.

My body is a rainbow vomited out of the
cloud. Around me are kingdoms made from

sunflowers & fresh lotus flowers, all making
an attempt at owning themselves.

References

Unger, R.M. [Chautauqua Institution] (Aug 5, 2014) "Krista Tippett with Roberto Mangabeira Unger."

Manuel, Carme. "The Day Of Doom and the Memory of Slavery: Octavia E. Butler's Prophetic Vision In Parable Of The Sower," n.d. /111.

Ransby, Barbara. *Ella Baker and the Black Freedom Movement.* Place of publication not identified: Readhowyouwant Com Ltd, 2012/173

Cone, James H. *The Cross and the Lynching Tree.* Maryknoll, NY: Orbis Books, 2019. /16

Keats, John, n.d./ Letters To J H Reynolds/ April 1817

Cramer, Jeffrey S. "Solid Seasons: the Friendship of Henry David Thoreau and Ralph Waldo Emerson." S.l.: COUNTERPOINT, 2020. ./225

Todorov, Tzvetan, and Richard Howard. *The Fantastic: a Structural Approach to a Literary Genre.* Ithaca, NY: Cornell Univ. Pr., 2007./ vii

Tuan, Yi-fu. *Morality and Imagination: Paradoxes of Progress.* Madison: University of Wisconsin Press, 1989./ 89, 90,

Scelfo, Julie. " On MLK Day, Honor the Mother of the Civil Rights Movement, Too." TIME.com, n.d. https://time.com/4633460/mlk-day-ella-baker/.

Miéville, China. "The Limits of Utopia." climateandcapitalism, n.d. https://climateandcapitalism.com/.

Theresa, Gaye, ed. *Futures Of Black Radicalism* , n.d. / 7

Du Bois, William Edward Burghardt. *The Gift of Black Folk: The Negroes in the Making of America,* n.d./ 135

Unger, R.M. [Big Think] (May 30, 2014) *Roberto Unger: Free Classical Social Theory from Illusions of False Necessity*

Unger, R.M [Art / Earth / Tech] (Aug 6, 2019) *Roberto Unger - February 2019*

Unger, R.M [Visions For The Future] (Jul 1, 2013) *The Origins of Roberto Mangabeira Unger's Philosophical Thought*

Bambara, Toni Cade. *The Salt Eaters*. London: Womens, 2000.

"The Power of Sankofa: Know History." Carter G. Wodson Center, n.d. https://www.berea.edu/cgwc/the-power-of-sankofa/.

Postman, Neil. *A Bridge to the Eighteenth Century*, n.d./ 5

Shelley, Percy. "In The Defense Of Poetry," n.d.

Kelley , Robin D.G. Freedom Dreams: The Making Of The Black Radical Tradition, n.d./158

Price, Richard. *Maroon Societies: Rebel Slave Communities in the Americas*, n.d.

Chicago Artists Coalition, n.d. https://chicagoartistscoalition.org/.

Weiner, Eric. *The Geography of Genius: a Search for the Worlds Most Creative Places, from Ancient Athens to Silicon Valley*. Farmington Hills, MI: Thorndike Press, 2016. / 74. 75.

Wolin, Sheldon S., and Nicholas Xenos. *Fugitive Democracy: and Other Essays*. Princeton, NJ: Princeton University Press, 2018. 107

Cesaire, Aime. *Discourse on Colonialism*. S.l.: Aakar Books, 2018. 82

Césaire Suzanne, Daniel Maximin, and Keith L. Walker. *The Great Camouflage: Writings of Dissent (1941-1945)*. Middletown, Conn: Wesleyan University Press, 2012.

Bois, Web Du. *Souls of Black Folk*. S.l.: Blurb, 2019.

Williams Clarence, Spencer. "Royal Garden Blues"/song 1919.

Butler, Octavia E. *Parable of the Talents*. New York: Grand Central Publishing, 2019.

Butler, Octavia E. *Parable of the Sower*. New York: Grand Central Publishing, 2019.

Butler, Octavia E., and Conseula Francis. *Conversations with Octavia Butler*. Jackson: University Press of Mississippi, 2010.

Hull, Gloria T. *Soul Talk: the New Spirituality of African American Women*. Rochester, VT: Inner Traditions, 2001.

Teish, Luisah. *Jambalaya: the Natural Womans Book of Personal Charms and Practical Rituals*. San Francisco: Harper & Row, 1988.

Marlowe, Lara. "Sarkozy Cancels Trip over Colonialism Protest." *The Irish Times*, n.d. https://www.irishtimes.com/news/sarkozy-cancels-trip-over-colonialism-protest-1.1172902.

Krebs, Albin. "Léopold Senghor Dies at 95; Senegal's Poet of Négritude." The *New York Times*, n.d. https://www.nytimes.com/2001/12/21/world/leopold-senghor-dies-at-95-senegal-s-poet-of-negritude.html.

Bogard, Paul. *End of Night: Searching for Natural Darkness in an Age of Artificial Light*. Harpercollins Publishers, 2014.

Perry, Imani. *Looking for Lorraine: the Radiant and Radical Life of Lorraine Hansberry*. Place of publication not identified. Beacon, 2019.

Jenkins, Andrea. *The T Is Not Silent*. Purple Lioness Productions 2015.

Perry, Imani [Princeton AAS] (Oct 27, 2016) "Imani Perry, Eddie S. Glaude, Jr., & Marc Lamont Hill in Conversation."

Unger, R.M. [Roberto Mangabeira Unger] (Feb 15, 2019) Conduct of Life Lecture February 13, 2019

"The Confucian Classics and The Civil Service Examination." http://afe.easia.columbia.edu/, n.d. http://afe.easia.columbia.edu/cosmos/irc/classics.htm.

About the Authors

Janel Cloyd is a poet, fiction writer, and essayist. She has been awarded a Willow Arts Alliance Residency with history concentration in the Weeksville African American Cultural Arts Center. She is a Watering Hole Poetry Fellow. She has been published in *Black Lives Have Always Mattered* (edited by Abiodun Oyewole of the Last Poets), *Mujeres*, *The Movement*, *The Muse Anthology*, *The Yellow Chair*, *Poeming Pigeon*, *Cave Canem Digital*, and *Gathering Round*. She is a 2017 finalist in the Peregrine Journal Pat Schneider Poetry Contest. Cloyd is a member of Women's Writer's Poetry in Bloom Poetry Salon and a member of the Poetry & Writer's Exchange. She is a mixed-media artist with a concentration in collage, paper arts, fiber, poetry, text, and images. Her work explores and embraces the themes of womanhood, spirituality, and the body aesthetic.

Adedayo Agarau is a Nigerian documentary photographer documenting the largest city in West Africa. He studies human nutrition and loves food like air. "When I was four, an older lady kissed me, and that was just the beginning," he says. "I am halved by water and memories."

Jermaine Thompson was born in Louisville, Mississippi. He learned language and wit from big-armed women who greased their skillets with gossip and from full-bellied men who cursed and prayed with the same fervor. He has an MFA in poetry from the University of Missouri–Kansas City, an MA in English from Mississippi State University, and BA in English from Stillman College. He has publications in *The Pinch*, *Memorious*, *Sprung Formal*, *Whale Road Review*, and *Southern Indiana Review*. He lives in Kansas City, Missouri, where he teaches ninth- and eleventh-grade English at Pembroke Hill Upper School and Introduction to Creative Writing at the University of Missouri–Kansas City.

Daniel B. Summerhill is an assistant professor of poetry/social action and composition studies at California State University, Monterey Bay.

He is the author of *Devine, Devine, Devine* (forthcoming), a semifinalist for the Charles B. Wheeler Poetry Prize. Summerhill holds an MFA in creative writing from Pine Manor College. He has received the Sharon Olds Fellowship and was nominated to Everipedia's 30 under 30 list. He is the 2015 New York Empire State Poetry Slam champion and a 2015 Nitty Gritty Grand Slam champion. His poems are published or forthcoming in the *Lilly Review, Califragle, Button, Blavity*, and elsewhere. A chapter of his research, "Black Voice; Cultivating Authentic Voice in Black Writers," was published by the Massachusetts Reading Association.

Melanie Henderson, a Washington, DC, native poet, editor, photographer, and publisher, is the author of *Elegies for New York Avenue*, winner of the 2011 Main Street Rag Poetry Book Award. An alumnus of Howard and Trinity Universities, she studied poetry at Howard University and at the Voices Summer Writing Workshops (VONA) in San Francisco, CA, prior to earning an MFA from Lesley University in Cambridge, MA. Her poems have appeared in *Beltway Poetry Quarterly, Drumvoices Revue, jubilat, Torch, Tuesday; An Art Project, Valley Voices, and the Washington Informer*, among others. She is a recipient of the 2009 Larry Neal Writers Award and received nominations for both the Pushcart Prize and the Orison Awards. She is a founding editor of *Tidal Basin Review*. Learn more at: www.dcelegies.com.

deziree a. brown is a black queer woman poet, scholar, and self-proclaimed social justice warrior, born and raised in Flint, Michigan. They are currently an MFA candidate at Northern Michigan University, and often claim to have been born with a poem written across their chest. A poetry and nonfiction editor for *Heavy Feather Review*, their work has appeared or is forthcoming in *BOAAT, decomP, Cartridge Lit, RHINO, Anomaly*, and the anthology *Best "New" African Poets 2015*, among others. They tweet at @deziree_a_brown.

Dominique "Mo" Durden is a twenty-two-year-old poet, avid reader, and lover of all things art. Her passion has always been music, poetry, and the arts as a whole. Poetry is her truth. Being able to find healing through her platform as an artist is a gift that she is truly thankful for. She can be found on social media platforms such as Twitter, Instagram, and Tumblr as @momothepoet.

Emiley Charley is first and foremost a black woman. Their love for their blackness, life, and love itself blossomed while attending Bowdoin College. Being surrounded by whiteness gave them absolutely no choice but to surrender to their blackness. It was then, in that moment of surrender, that they came home to themselves.

Latif Askia Ba was born on August 17, 1998, in New York City with dyskinetic cerebral palsy. He grew up in Brooklyn and Staten Island. He currently is a senior at Edinboro University, majoring in computer science with a minor in mathematics and creative writing.. He plans on using his degree to become a game developer.

Eric Lawing lives, works, and writes in Freeport, New York. Lawing is an avid reader, anime/hip-hop enthusiast, and crate digger/hoarder of vinyl records. Lawing is currently studying literature at Adelphi University.

Evelyn Burroughs, an African American poet, was born and raised in the Midwest. A retired composition and literature teacher, she currently lives and writes in San Diego. Several of her poems have appeared in local journals: *The Forum*, *1995*, *San Diego Poetry Anthology*, and *A Year in Ink*.

Evyan Roberts (she/her) is a queer, fat, black femme who is deeply committed to intersectional feminism and #blackgirlmagic. Her writing has appeared in *Ithaca Lit*, *Not Your Mother's Breast Milk*, *Rogue Agent*, and *Kissing Dynamite*, where she was the featured poet for August 2019, and elsewhere. She is currently living in Silver Spring, Maryland, and pursuing a master's in social work.

Lester Batiste is a savage writer in living color who is originally from Chicago, Illinois. He holds an MFA from the University of Southern

Maine, as well as a master's of education from the University of Pennsylvania. Lester lives in North Minneapolis, Minnesota, and teaches English classes at an independent high school. When he is not teaching, Lester enjoys writing in multiple genres from poetry to creative nonfiction, playing sports, and watching television.

Grace C. Ocasio has appeared or is forthcoming in the *Chaffin Journal*, *Rattle*, *Black Renaissance Noire*, *Court Green*, *Minerva Rising*, and elsewhere. Ocasio is originally from New York. Their honors include a nomination for the Pushcart Prize in 2016, placing as a finalist in the 2016 Aesthetica Creative Writing Award for Poetry, receiving the 2014 North Carolina Arts Council Regional Artist Project Grant, winning honorable mention in the 2012 James Applewhite Poetry Prize, winning the 2011 Sonia Sanchez and Amiri Baraka Prize in Poetry, and becoming a scholarship recipient to the 2011 Napa Valley Writers' Conference.

Irene Vázquez is a junior at Yale, where she is the managing editor of *Broad Recognition*, Yale's feminist publication, as well as the copresident of WORD: Performance Poetry at Yale. She is interested in the poetics of redress, belonging, and global liberation, generally through the lens of Black studies. Irene is a Pushcart Prize–nominated writer. Her works have appeared or are forthcoming in the *Houston Chronicle*, *Alexandria Quarterly*, and *F(r)iction*, among others. Mostly she likes drinking coffee, watching *Dear White People*, and pointing out the differences between her Yale experience and Rory Gilmore's. Her work can be found at www.irenevazquez.com.

Namir Fearce is an interdisciplinary artist residing in Chicago by way of North Minneapolis. Fluidity is central to his practice, drawing on a constellation of references and sites of Black American queer experience. He uses these histories, both personal and cultural, to weave complex, emotional, and political landscapes while exploring the potential bodies, identities, and stories that can arise in these newly woven spaces. Fearce is a fourth-year BFA candidate at the School of Art & Art History at the University of Illinois at Chicago. His work has been featured in Red

Bull Music Academy, *Paper* magazine, the Museum of Contemporary Art Chicago, the Walker Art Center, the Soap Factory, and more.

Ivy Irihamye loves pretty much everything that loves back, including but not limited to: the environment, people, words, and cheesecake. Ivy, as of right now, is a student at Centre College in (Central) Kentucky; her parents are originally from Kigali, Rwanda, and she calls Lexington, Kentucky, her hometown. She has little educational merit to her name yet, but does have a high school diploma from the Gatton Academy at Western Kentucky University. Ivy founded the Fayette Youth Writing and Arts Competition and has been involved in a couple literary magazines. She is currently involved in Centre College's literary magazine *Vantage Point* but is mostly really trying very hard to pass her classes. You can find some of Ivy's work at @ivydoeslanguage on Instagram.

Julian Randall is a living Queer, Black poet from Chicago. He has received fellowships from *Callaloo*, *BOAAT*, and the *Watering Hole*, and was the 2015 National College Slam (CUPSI) Best Poet. Julian is the curator of *Winter Tangerine Review*'s Lineage of Mirrors. His work has appeared or is forthcoming in publications such as *New York Times Magazine*, *The Georgia Review* and *Sixth Finch* and in the anthologies *Portrait in Blues*, *Nepantla*, and *New Poetry from the Midwest*. He is a candidate for his MFA in poetry at Ole Miss. His first book, *Refuse*, is the winner of the 2017 Cave Canem Poetry prize and will be published by University of Pittsburgh Press in Fall 2018.

Kemi Alabi is a free blk shapeshifter. Author of *The Lion Tamer's Daughter* (YesYes Books, 2020), their poetry and essays have many homes, including *Guernica*, *The Rumpus*, *Catapult*, *the Guardian*, *The BreakBeat Poets Vol. 2* (Haymarket Press, 2018), and *Best New Poets 2019* (University of Virginia Press, 2019). As culture strategy director of Forward Together, Kemi leads Echoing Ida, a community of Black women and nonbinary writers. They live in Chicago, Illinois.

Kateema Lee is a Washington, DC, native. Her recent work has been published in print and online journals such as *Beltway Poetry Quarterly*,

African American Review, *Gargoyle*, *Baltimore Review*, and others. Kateema is the author of two chapbooks, *Almost Invisible* and *Musings of a Netflix Binge Viewer*. Her forthcoming collection, *Black Random* (July 2020), explores joy, identity, violence, and the "brief, bright lives" of missing and forgotten black women in the District of Columbia.

khaliah d. pitts is a Philly native and a lifelong artist. A writer and food educator, she dedicates her work to telling the stories of brown people and always striving for liberation. In 2016, she co-created *Our Mothers' Kitchens Culinary + Literature Project* for girls of color with her sister-friend, Shivon Love.

LaShawn Smith-Wright is a college freshman who is originally from Detroit, MI. They are a competitive slam poet who has competed twice at Brave New Voices Youth Poetry Slam.

Maroula Blades is an Afro-British poet, writer, and painter living in Berlin. She is currently nominated for the Amadeu Antonio Prize 2019 for her multimedia poetry project "Fringe." She received a High Honorable Mention in the 2019 Stephen A. Dibase Poetry Contest Awards and was the first runner-up in the 2018 Tony Quagliano International Poetry Award and the winner of the Caribbean Writer 2014 Flash Fiction Competition and the Erbacce Poetry Prize 2012. Her first poetry collection, *Blood Orange*, is published by Erbacce-press. Works have been published in *Stories of Music 2*, *The Freshwater Review*, *Thrice Fiction*, *Volume Magazine*, the *London Reader*, *So It Goes: The Journal of the Kurt Vonnegut Memorial Library*, *Theories of HER* anthology, *Abridged*, the *Caribbean Writer*, *Trespass Magazine*, *Words with Jam*, *Blackberry Magazine*, the *Latin Heritage Foundation*, and *Peepal Tree Press*, among others. Her poetry/music/art programs have been presented on several German stages.

Lisa Marie Brimmer (she/her) is a queer, black, transracial adoptee activist, performance artist, and writer. She has been published in literary magazines such as *Ishmael Reed's Konch Magazine*, *Gazillion Voices*, *On the Commons Magazine*, and *Burn Something Zine*, and has been included in multiple anthologies. She is co-editor of Minnesota Historical Society Press's *Queer Voices of Minnesota* (2019). Brimmer is a two-time Givens Foundation for African American Literature fellow and has received a Many Voices Fellowship for playwriting at the Playwright's Center in Minneapolis. Brimmer is graduate fellow at University of St. Thomas in St. Paul, Minnesota, where she received her master's degree in English literature (2018). Her work has been presented in panels at Split This Rock! in Washington, DC (2018), and the Center for Multi-Ethnic Studies: Europe and the Americas (MESEA) in Graz, Austria (2018).

Lauren Fields is a third-year medical student in New York, though she continues to write poetry as a means of grappling with, exploring, and celebrating what it means to be an African-American woman living in the United States. Her poems have been published in *Blackberry: A Magazine, Linden Avenue Literary Journal, WATER Literary and Arts Magazine, and Reflexions Literary and Fine Arts Journal* of CUIMC.

May Livere's poetry and short stories have been published on Africanwriter.com, *Angie's Diary, Fiction on the Web*, and *Africa Book Club*. Her short story "Lemayian's Invention" was a first runner-up for the September 2013 Africa Book Club Short Reads competition, and was subsequently published in Africa Book Club's first anthology *The Bundle of Joy and Other Stories from Africa* (2014).

Ashley Davis is aCalifornia born and raised, New York–educated, Boston-bred, Philly-based black queer, womxn, poet, and educator whose work is personal and performed with the intention to connect to those around her in order to build community and continue healing. Ashley was a part of the VONA 2017 cohort facilitated by Patricia Smith, was a part of the 2016 Finalist team "House Slam" at the National Poetry Slam, and was a finalist for the 2016 National Underground Individual Poetry Competition. She currently lives with her grandmother and great-grandmother connecting to her spirit guides, learning her craft, and protecting her energy.

Maya Angelique is a twenty-one-year-old writer from southern New Jersey who specializes in poetry and prose. Their first poetry collection, *Water Comes First*, is available now on Amazon.com. From the age of nine, they have used writing poetry as a means of coping with adverse forces. They're an advocate for self-love and awareness, mental wellness, women who have suffered from abuse, and spiritual connection to one's heritage. Their work has been featured on the Spelman College chapter of *The Odyssey Online*, as well as *NEA Today* (you will find them under Maya Elie). They have also been selected to perform at the annual Decatur Book Festival in 2016 on behalf of Spelman College and assisted in conducting poetry workshops for children at Dunbar Elementary School in Atlanta, Georgia.

Maurisa Li-A-Ping is an Afro-Caribbean Black Queer Woman. She is a storyteller and educator raised by a village of Black women in Brooklyn, New York. Maurisa utilizes poetry to promote the success of marginalized students on college campuses through collectivist, culturally validating spaces. Maurisa's commitment to higher education and craft has allowed her to perform and present at the Herman C. Hudson Symposium, NASPA Conference, ACPA Convention, the National Conference on Student Leadership (NCSL), the North Avenue Knowledge Exchange, and more. Her performances have allowed her to touch stages at the world-famous Apollo Theater, United Nations, Poetic License Festival, Barclay Center, and more. Her dedication to her craft has led her to receive the Ernst Pawel Award for literary excellence and national and regional honors from the Scholastic Art and Writing Awards. Maurisa is a recent graduate from Indiana University and has (forthcoming) publication in *Black Diasporas*, *Lunch Ticket*, and *Wusgood Mag*.

Maya Williams (she/hers and they/them) is a mixed-race black suicide survivor and writer residing in Portland, Maine. She has published poetry in spaces such as *glitterMOB*, *Occulum*, *Portland Press Herald*, *Frost Meadow Review*, *Homology Lit*, and more. They have published essays in spaces such as *The Tempest, Black Youth Project, and The Trill Project*. They were also a semifinalist for Nimrod International Journal's 2018

Francine Ringold Award for New Writers. Follow her @emmdubb16 on Twitter and Instagram, and at mayawilliamspoet.com.

Derek D. Brown is a poet and spoken word artist from Los Angeles, California. They are the author of *Articulate Scars: Comfortable Silences and Reluctant Tears* from Still Water Publishing, available at www.derekdbrown.com. Their poems have also been published in several anthologies, most recently the highly anticipated *Voices from Leimert Park: Redux* from Harriet Tubman Press.

Millicent Campbell is a speech-language pathologist, poet, and writer living in Houston, Texas. Millicent works in the public school system helping children with language differences communicate. She is currently working on her debut poetry collection that intertwines her Southern heritage, race, gender, and faith.

mia s. willis is an African American artist and adventurer born in Charlotte, North Carolina. I have been a spoken word poet since my introduction to the art in 2013. I am currently a member of North Carolina's the Marquis Slam, a Poetry Slam, Inc. collective that ranked in the top twenty teams in the nation at the 2017 National Poetry Slam. My work has been featured in print by East Carolina University's *Expressions* magazine and *SUGAR*, respectively, as well as online by *Fem Lit Mag*, *INTER*, and *a feminist thread*. My visual album of poetry, titled *Sage and Petrichor*, was released on YouTube in September 2017.

Mekleit Dix lives in Ladera Heights, California. Dix is attending Loyola Marymount University for a dual degree candidate for English and biology, and a minor in women's and gender studies.

Nicole Lawrence is a Bronx-bred island gyal who teaches by day and navigates worlds by pen at night.

Nome Emeka Patrick is a student in the University of Benin, Nigeria, where he studies English language and literature. His works have been published or forthcoming in *POETRY*, *Poet Lore*, *Strange*

Horizons, *Beloit Poetry Journal*, *Notre Dame Review*, *Puerto Del Sol*, *FLAPPERHOUSE*, *Gargouille*, *Crannóg*, *Mud Season Review*, *Oakland Review*, *Barnhouse Journal*, *Up the Staircase Quarterly*, and elsewhere. His manuscript *We Need New Moses. Or New Luther King* was a finalist for the 2018 Sillerman First Book Prize for African Poets. He is currently guest-editing, alongside Itiola Jones, *Nigerian Young Poets Anthology*. He lives in a small room close to banana trees and bird songs in Benin, where he writes and studies for his final exams in the university.

O'Phylia Smiley is a poet living in lower Alabama. Her work has been published in *Occulum*, and she has forthcoming work in *Heather Press*. When she's not writing, she's reading, and when she's not reading, she's yelling on Twitter about chinchillas. She can be found @ophyliaXhamlet.

paul singleton iii (b. 1982 Fort Campbell, KY) is a multidisciplinary artist whose work brings together poetry, book making, and origami as methods of contemplative inquiry. His work has appeared in *Maple Leaf Rag*, *Invisible Bear* (Duke University), and *Break/Water Review*. Currently paul is working towards his master of science degree in Chinese medicine. You can follow paul on social media @joyfulbrave

Olivia Dorsey Peacock is a technologist from North Carolina who currently lives in Dallas, Texas, with her husband. By day, she helps doctors and academics make sense of health data; by night, she unravels genealogical mysteries. She has a bachelor's and a master's of information science from the University of North Carolina at Chapel Hill. When she's not writing poetry, she's using technology to craft solutions that elevate and amplify African American history and genealogy.

Shavonna Walker is a queer Black woman from Compton, California. She is currently a special education teacher serving children with a variety of learning disabilities in historically disenfranchised communities of color. Her current work was greatly shaped by her undergraduate experience at UC Santa Barbara, where she earned her bachelor's degrees in feminist studies and psychology. When she is not working, she is writing for solace, self-care, and survival.

Tara Betts is a Chicago-based poet and the author of *Break the Habit* and *Arc & Hue*, as well as the chapbooks *7 x 7: kwansabas* and *THE GREATEST!: An Homage to Muhammad Ali*. She is part of the MFA faculty at Stonecoast, University of Southern Maine. In addition to her work as the poetry editor at *Another Chicago Magazine* and the Langston *Hughes Review*, she signed on as the lit editor at *Newcity* and the editor at *Beautiful People*.

Taylor Scott is a First Wave alumni. She has a master's in English from Louisiana State University and is currently a teaching artist with Forward Arts, a nonprofit specializing in youth poetry and programming. She knows every Nina Simone song and spends too much money on food.

Salaam Green is an award-winning poet and author, the 2016 Poet Laureate for Innovation and Entrepreneurship, a 2019 Reimagine Justice fellow and TEDx alumni, and daughter of Alabama's Black Belt. As owner and founder of TheLiteraryHealingArts.com and Red Couch Writers, she can be found helping others write to heal on red couches across the city of Birmingham, Alabama. She is a 2019 New Economy Coalition Climate Solutions Fellow and an advocate for environmental and restorative justice in rural Alabama. A writer and storyteller, her work has appeared in the *Birmingham Times*, *Scalawag*, *Bust*, *Feminist Review*, *Black Youth Project*, *Elephant Journal*, *Southern Women's Review*, *AL.com*, *Birmingham Arts Journal*, and more.

Tayo Omisore is a poet, singer-songwriter, and undergraduate accounting student at the University of Maryland. His work is forthcoming in *Stylus* and *Up the Staircase Quarterly*. His poems "Scouting Report" and "Cover of UGK's International Players' Anthem" were both finalists for the 2018 Jiménez-Porter Literary Prize.

Quartez Harris spent much of his educational experience with an Individual Education Program (IEP) due to disabilities in comprehension skills and writing expression. Not long after graduating from college, he competed in the Second Annual Grand Tournament Competition hosted by Writing Knights Press. His prize was a full-length book deal. Harris·released his first book of poetry, *Nothing but Skin*, in 2014.

Tumelo Cassandra Twala is a nineteen-year-old South African poet currently in her second year of university at the University of Cape Town.

Jorrell Watkins (Brotha Jorrell) is an educator and interdisciplinary artist from Richmond, VA. He earned his BA from Hampshire College. From 2014–2017, he served as the director of the nationally touring hip-hop theater play, *Mixed Race Mixtape*. He was a 2018 National Young Playwright in Residence at the Echo Theater Company, and a 2019 VQR Scholar in Poetry at the VQR's Writing Conference in Charlottesville, VA. His poetry is published/forthcoming in *Obsidian*, *The Amistad Journal*, *Juke Joint Magazine*, and elsewhere. Currently, he is a MFA poetry candidate at the Iowa Writers' Workshop at the University of Iowa. Find him on Instagram and Twitter @brothajorrell.

Quintin Collins is a poet, managing editor, and Solstice MFA program candidate from the Chicago area who currently lives in Boston. His works have appeared or are forthcoming in *Threshold*, *Glass Mountain*, *Eclectica*, *Transition*, and elsewhere. If he were to have one extravagance, it would be a personal sommelier to give him wine pairings for books.

Patience Imolele is a poet living in London, England. Born in Nigeria, her experience as a young black woman inspires much of her poetry, exploring themes such as love, identity, and family. When she was young she loved to write and would make up stories constantly. Going on to study law at university, she found her way back to writing and since graduating has been able to dedicate herself to it more fully.

Alexus Erin is originally from Princeton, New Jersey, and is currently living in Manchester, UK, where she is a PhD candidate. Her written work specializes in the theoretical frameworks of embodiment, as well as feminist, gender, critical race, and environmental justice studies. Her poetry has previously appeared in *Potluck Magazine*, the *Melanin Collective*, *The Nervous Breakdown*, *The Audacity* (audacityzine.com), the *American Society of Young Poets*, and a host of others. Erin's two chapbooks, *Two Birds, All Moon* and *St. John's Wort* were published by Gap Riot Press and Animal Heart Press, respectively. Her screenplay, *American Lotus Project*, won an award at Temple University's Diamond Film Festival.

Ricardo Lowe Jr., also known as Rico, is a poet and scholar of West Indian descent. He was born a military brat in Laughlin AFB, Texas, and has lived in Panama, England, and Denver, Colorado, prior to settling down in San Antonio, Texas. Much of Rico's creative work is devoted to black identity.

Salisa Grant is a poet and educator from Duluth, Minnesota. She is a doctoral student at Howard University, an English professor, and currently resides in the Washington, DC, area. Her poems can be found in her debut poetry collection, *In These Black Hands* (2019).

Victor A. Kwansa is an attorney, education advocate, poet, and essayist from Prince George's County, Maryland. They received a BA in political science from Yale University in 2008 and graduated from Harvard Law School in 2011. Their essays have been featured in the *Huffington Post*, *Blavity*, and a Yale booklet for incoming freshmen. Their poetry has been featured in *Essence*, *CURA: A Literary Magazine of Art and Action*, and Yale's student publication, *Sphere*. In 2010, they were featured in *The Root*'s online gallery of up-and-coming artists and entrepreneurs.

Valérie Déus is a poet and film curator. Her work has been featured in the *Brooklyn Rail*, *Midway*, *Aforementioned Productions*, the *St. Paul Almanac*, and most recently in the *BeZine*. Her chapbook, *Skull-Filled Sun*, is available on Amazon. She is the host of Project 35, a local low-fi radio show featuring poetry and music. She curates Film North's Cinema Lounge and is the shorts programmer for the Provincetown International Film Festival.

Simone-Marie Feigenbaum is twenty-eight years old, born and raised in Brooklyn, New York. They are currently an ELA teacher at the Bronx High School for Medical Science. They have a BA in English from Allegheny College and an MFA from American University. They have been published on the Shakespeare Theatre Company website as part of their Poets-In-Residence series, on the *Ms. Magazine* "Ms. Muse" page as part of their Independence Day Special, and on Button Poetry's Instagram page for their short format competition. More of their writing can be found on their Instagram page, @writemagick.

Brittany Marshall was the 2016–17 Youth Poet Laureate of Baton Rouge, Louisiana. Her collection *musings of a black girl* was published May 2017 by Penmanship Books; it is a series of poetic meditations that reveal attempts to grow out of the legacies of home and homelands. She is currently a public-school English teacher, building relationships with her twelfth-graders one shady comment at a time.

Wálé Àyìnlá is a twenty-year-old Nigerian writer and poet who writes from the ancient city of Abeokuta. His works appear or are forthcoming in *Brittle Paper, Kalahari Review, Prachya Review, Dwarts, Expound,* and others. His poem "Little Boys are Large Exit Doors" was a finalist in the Kreative Diadem Poetry Prize, 2017. He is @Wale_Ayinla on Twitter.

Black Table Arts is an emerging arts organization that conjures other worlds through black art by connecting communities and cultivating volume in black life. Located in Minneapolis, Minnesota, Black Table Arts puts black joy on legs and walks it into the living room of the future. It grows community through public programming such as the Black Lines Matter writing classroom at the Loft Literary Center and the Because Black Life Conference.